Macmillan Geography

General editors:
Keith Orrell and Harry Tolley

Population and Development

Chris Warn and Peter Wilby

Macmillan Education

First published 1984
Reprinted 1986, 1987

Published by
MACMILLAN EDUCATION LTD
Houndmills, Basingstoke, Hampshire RG21 2XS
and London
Companies and representatives
throughout the world

Printed in Great Britain by
Bath Press
Bath

ISBN 0-333-27642-6

Contents

Preface

In recent years rapid changes in Geography have left teachers with a wide, almost bewildering choice of content and methodology for inclusion in their courses. Thus in devising this series and advising on each text we, the editors, have had regard for the needs of pupils and the general educational aims of schooling as well as the evolving nature of the subject.

The series is intended primarily for 14–16 year olds studying for O level and CSE examinations, though it may be used profitably with students following new sixth form courses. As editors, we have been aware of likely shifts in the examination system at 16 + and have tried to include the best of what Geography has to offer the school curriculum at this level. Specifically, we think the subject can contribute to a greater understanding of the pupils' real world experience, their acquisition of a sense of place, the development in them of an environmental ethic and an empathy with people from different cultures and in other societies. Additionally, Geography can aid the development of literacy, numeracy and graphicacy as well as intellectual and social skills. These subject specific and general goals have been used as criteria in the writing and editing of this series.

The series presents a diversity of resources on which exercises have been based to demonstrate the principles of enquiry in Geography and to promote general study skills and competence. We have tried to match the reading level of the text to the abilities of 14–16 age groups. An appropriate geographical vocabulary has been deliberately introduced and defined in each of the texts.

The topics which are covered within the five titles in the series are the ones which, in the opinion of the authors and editors, have greatest relevance to the future lives of pupils. We have tried to demonstrate how the geographer's view can contribute to an understanding of issues and problems at a variety of scales in a diversity of locations.

The closely related themes of population and development raise many of the most vital questions facing society today. In *Population and Development*, Chris Warn and Peter

Wilby demonstrate how students can use the geographer's approach to analyse and understand these problems and issues which have a growing influence on their daily lives. The authors have taken great care to establish a sound and appropriate conceptual framework within which these problems can be considered. The straightforward language and basic geographical vocabulary make a readable text ideal for first examination courses. Methods of study using various quantitative techniques and model-based approaches have also been integrated into the text. The outstanding feature of the book, however, is the use the authors have made of original resource material for exercises and discussion. This text will undoubtedly help students clarify their values and attitudes in this important area of study.

A crowd flowed over London Bridge, so many
I had not thought death had undone so many.

T. S. Eliot *The Waste Land*

1 Population patterns

Population debated
Lords urge action

Advocating an increase in the £5½ million currently allocated annually to family planning overseas, Lord Ritchie Calder warned the House yesterday "We are looking without question at a situation which, if it goes on, will be totally and completely disastrous. The numbers game does not mean anything."

figure 1.1 Newspaper report on a House of Lords debate in 1979. The government was being urged to spend more on population control

We all have our own ideas about population, its size, distribution, characteristics and behaviour. We debate it in newspapers, on TV and in public places. Our government produces policies to influence how many of us there will be in the future (fig. 1.1). And yet there are few of us who have any real idea how many people there are in the world.

The above paragraph presents an idea in a persuasive form and leads you to a statement which you are intended to accept. But you should look upon such statements as the ideas of other people — ideas which need to be tested. You can test these ideas quickly against what you already know to be true, or you can undertake a simple piece of research. In this case you could conduct a survey to test the statement that 'few of us have any real idea how many people there are in the world'; in other words, 'people's perceptions of population size are erratic'.

How many of us are there?

A group of students asked their colleagues, parents and teachers the question 'How many people are there in the world?'

The replies were plotted on a **dispersion diagram** (fig. 1.2) which shows the spread of the replies. Notice that the scale which the students constructed did not allow the highest guesses to be plotted: they did not expect such very high estimates.

The highest estimate was one million million.

The lowest estimate was one hundred million.

The difference between these two extremes is the **range** — 999 900 million.

The most frequent reply, the **mode**, was 4000 million.

But the mode, although the most popular guess, was the choice of only eight of the forty-five people in the survey. The diagram shows that 37 of the 45 guesses (i.e. over 80 per

1

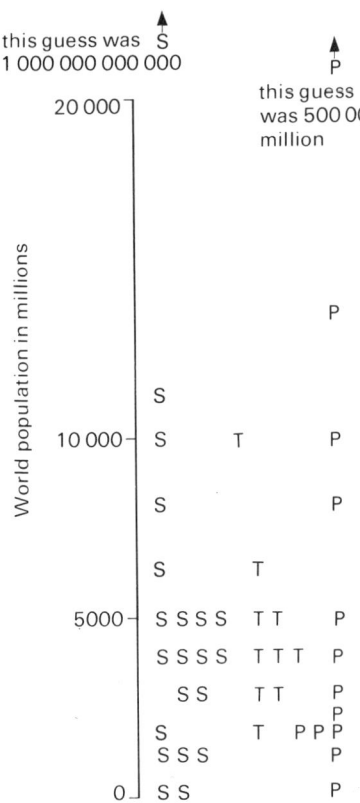

this guess was S
1 000 000 000 000

this guess was 500 000 million

World population in millions

figure 1.2 Dispersion diagram: estimates of total world population by students (S), teachers (T) and parents (P)

figure 1.3 Just a part of a crowd of 50 000 football supporters in Anfield Stadium

cent of them) differ from the mode by more than 1000 million. The survey therefore supports the statement that people's perceptions of population size are erratic: their guesses are all over the place!

If people are asked to estimate the size of population of their own country, even their own town, they can be very wide of the mark. It seems as if people have clear ideas about population size only when they are dealing with small units which they have actually experienced.

Most people can visualise a football crowd like the one in the photo (fig 1.3) so they have some idea what 50 000 people look like shoulder to shoulder.

Almost everyone has some experience of a town like that in figs 1.4 and 1.5 so they have a good idea what 50 000 people look like in the landscape: in their houses, factories, schools, offices .... You should compare the size of this town of 50 000 people with the towns near your home. To do this you can use the AA or RAC handbooks (see fig. 1.6).

We rarely 'experience' people in larger numbers than the football crowd or small town. But if we live in or visit a large city such as Edinburgh or Leeds we can attach some meaning to 500 000 (half a million) people. The city in fig. 1.7 has ten times the population of the town in fig. 1.5.

table 1.1   World population by continents and countries with over 50 million people (source: 1981 World Bank Atlas)

Continent		Countries with over 50 million people	
Asia	2500 million	China	982 million
		India	660 million
		Indonesia	143 million
		Japan	116 million
		Bangladesh	88 million
		Pakistan	80 million
		Vietnam	53 million
	265 million	USSR	265 million
Europe (excluding USSR)	520 million	West Germany	61 million
		United Kingdom	56 million
		France	53 million
Africa	470 million	Nigeria	84 million
Latin America	360 million	Brazil	116 million
North America	250 million	USA	224 million
Oceania	23 million		
World total	4400 million		

Beyond this size we have to rely on our imagination. But at least we have some foundation on which to build our perceptions of larger population units such as the states of Europe. France and the United Kingdom each have more than 50 000 000 (fifty million) people. How many Edinburghs does this represent? You can see in table 1.1 the names of all the countries in the world with a population of over 50 million.

figure 1.4 Fifty thousand people in the landscape, in their houses, schools, offices, shops, factories . . .

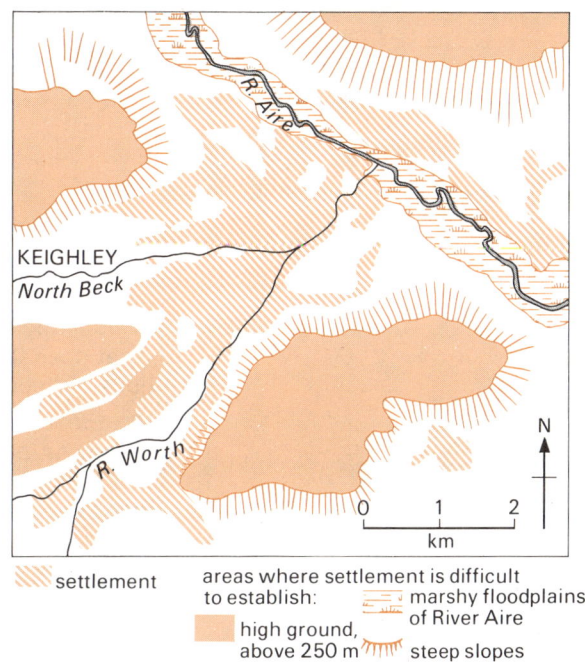

KEIGHLEY
North Beck

R. Worth

R. Aire

N

0   1   2
          km

|||| settlement

areas where settlement is difficult to establish:

high ground, above 250 m

marshy floodplains of River Aire

steep slopes

figure 1.5 Map of the town and surrounding country shown in fig. 1.4

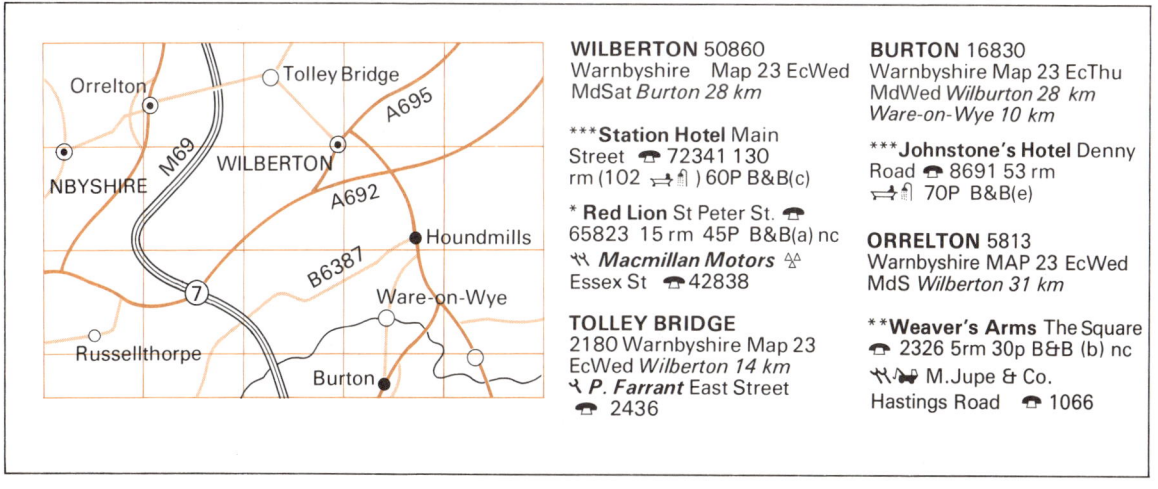

Orrelton
Tolley Bridge
A695
M69
WILBERTON
NBYSHIRE
A692
Houndmills
B6387
7
Ware-on-Wye
Russellthorpe
Burton

WILBERTON 50860
Warnbyshire   Map 23 EcWed
MdSat *Burton 28 km*

******Station Hotel** Main
Street ☎ 72341 130
rm (102 ⇥🛁) 60P B&B(c)

* Red Lion St Peter St. ☎
65823 15 rm 45P B&B(a) nc

🔧 *Macmillan Motors* ⚙
Essex St ☎42838

TOLLEY BRIDGE
2180 Warnbyshire Map 23
EcWed *Wilberton 14 km*
🔧 *P. Farrant* East Street
☎ 2436

BURTON 16830
Warnbyshire Map 23 EcThu
MdWed *Wilburton 28 km*
Ware-on-Wye 10 km

***Johnstone's Hotel Denny
Road ☎ 8691 53 rm
⇥🛁 70P B&B(e)

ORRELTON 5813
Warnbyshire MAP 23 EcWed
MdS *Wilberton 31 km*

**Weaver's Arms The Square
☎ 2326 5rm 30p B&B (b) nc

🔧🚗 M.Jupe & Co.
Hastings Road ☎ 1066

figure 1.6 A map of the kind found in AA and RAC handbooks and gazetteer entries for three towns shown on the map

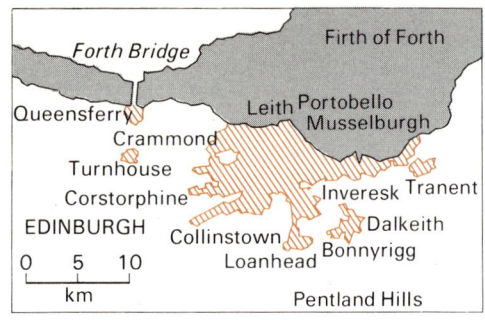

figure 1.7 Map of Edinburgh, a city of about 500 000 inhabitants

Note carefully the different scales of figs. 1.5 and 1.7. Which other British cities have over half a million people?

Our imagination must now make a big jump to the 'super powers' of USA and USSR with over two hundred million (200 000 000) each. And, finally, a mind-bending leap takes us to the world's total population — to more than 4 000 000 000 (four thousand million).

These are difficult figures to visualise. The exercises which follow suggest some helpful methods of sharpening and refining people's perceptions of population size — they give us a clearer idea of the numbers involved.

Exercises

1 *Either* conduct a survey of your class, relations, teachers and neighbours, asking them how many people they think there are in the world. Draw a dispersion diagram as in fig. 1.2.
Or copy the dispersion diagram in fig. 1.2.
What does the dispersion diagram tell you about people's perceptions of population size?

2 *Either* find the size of the towns in your home region (you could use an AA or RAC book from home or library), *or* use the information in fig. 1.6 to do this exercise:
Plot the towns on a sketch map, showing each town as a circle whose size is proportional to the size of the town's population. Make an estimate of the size of the population of the whole area shown on your sketch map.

3 Use the statistics in table 1.1 to do these exercises:
(a) Copy fig. 1.8 and complete it, marking off first the continents and then the countries.
(b) Copy and complete fig. 1.9 to show the relative size of each continent's population.
(c) Show the statistics by some other means (e.g. by drawing vertical columns of different heights to show the populations of the continents).

4 Figures 1.8 to 1.11 show some different methods of representing the same information. Study them together with the graph you drew for question 3(c). Giving comments and reasons:
(a) Which shows most clearly the difference between Europe and Asia?
(b) Which is the best for showing that Asia has 100 times more people than Oceania?
(c) Which shows most clearly that Asia has over half the world's total population?
(d) Which method is most eye-catching?
(e) Which is most accurate?
(f) Which is most interesting?
(g) Which is easiest to construct?
(h) Which is actually misleading?
(i) Taking into consideration all you have done in this question, which method do you think best overall?

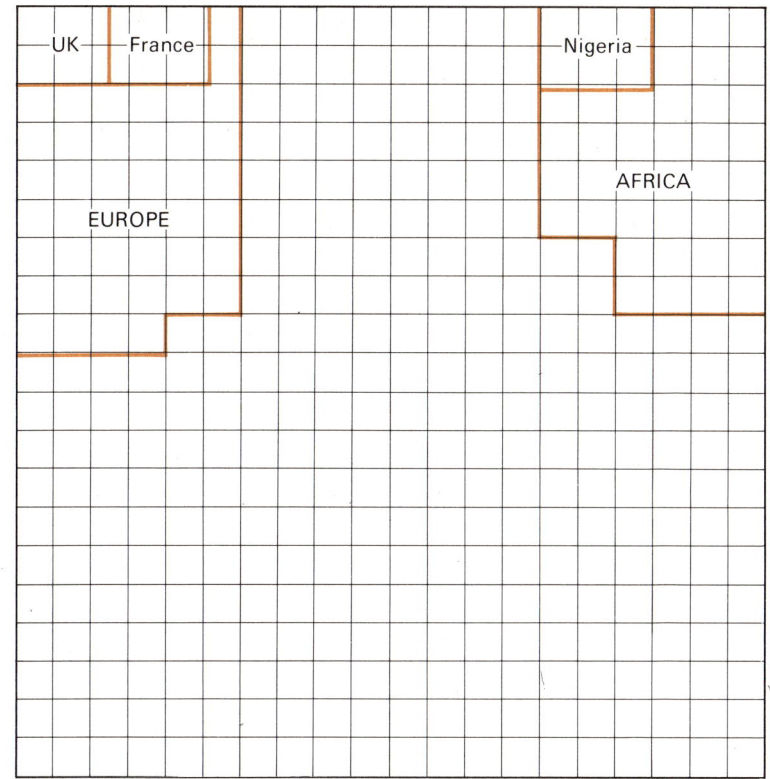

figure 1.8 World population diagram. Each square □ represents ten million people. The whole diagram represents the world total

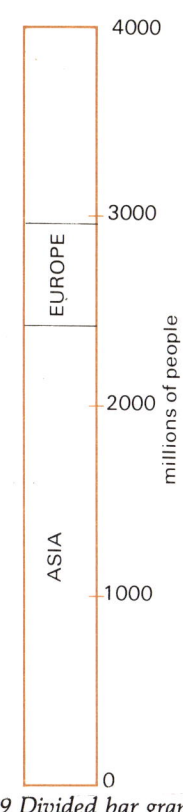

figure 1.9 Divided bar graph of world population

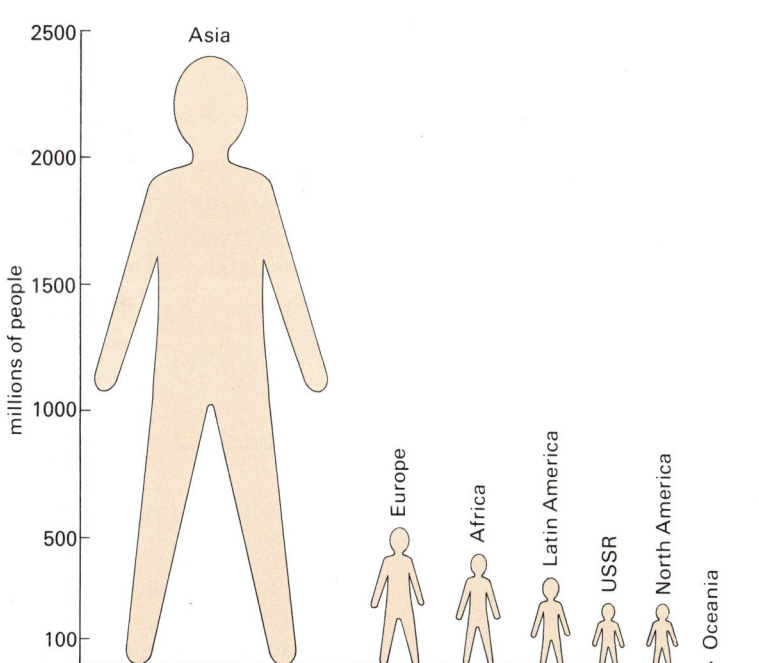

figure 1.10 **Isotype** *showing populations of major world regions*

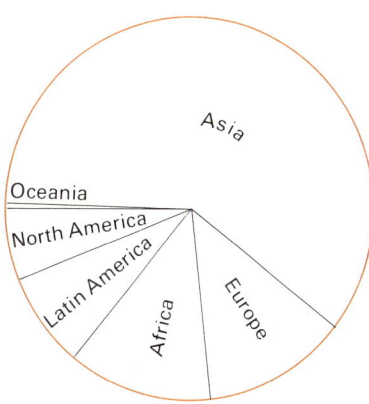

figure 1.11 Pie chart or segmented circle, showing world population by continents

5 Use the information in table 1.1 to mark and name on a world outline map all the countries with populations over 50 000 000. If a duplicated map is not available use fig. 11.3 (p. 106) to make a tracing. Make a list of the ten countries with the largest population, ranking them according to size.

6 Try to update the statistics you have been using (your sources may include *The World Bank Atlas*, newspaper articles, newly published reference books).

Where is everybody?

It should by now be clear what we mean by 'population'. You may use the word in Biology to mean 'a group of plants or animals'. But in Geography it refers to *people*. The noun 'population' derives from the Latin word 'populus' meaning 'a people'. In Geography we consider not only *how many* there are but also *where* they are.

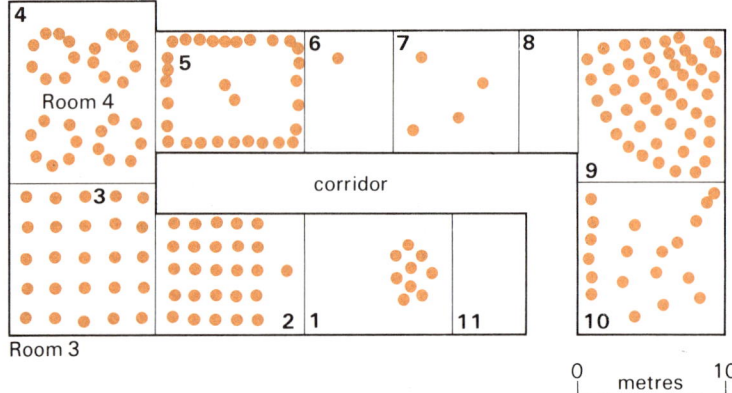

figure 1.12 Plan of part of a school, showing the distribution of people at a particular moment

A plan of your school at this very moment might show patterns similar to fig. 1.12, if you showed every person's position with a dot. A few moments later the picture will change. But at this moment every space around the school has its own population characteristics:

1. Some rooms contain more people than others. This is a simple matter of **population size**.
2. Some rooms are more crowded than others. This is a question of **population density**.

   You will measure density in science as *the amount of something relative to the space it occupies*, i.e., mass divided by volume, $m \div v$, $\frac{m}{v}$. In **demography** (the study of population) we measure density of population as the number of people relative to the space they

occupy, i.e., number of people divided by the area,
$n \div a, \dfrac{n}{a}$.

In fig. 1.12 we can see that rooms 3 and 4 are of different size (room 3 = 100 square metres, room 4 = 120 square metres),
and they contain different numbers of people (room 3 = 25, room 4 = 30),
but both have the same density (0.25 per square metre — check this for yourself).

3. If you compare rooms 3 and 4 you will see that the people in the rooms are spread out differently. Although they have the same density they have different patterns of **distribution**.

In one of the rooms the distribution of people is perfectly **regular**. Each person is precisely one metre from his nearest neighbour and the whole room is evenly occupied. The pupils are spread out in this way because they are taking an exam. You may be able to think of parts of Europe where the landscape is laid out in this geometric way and the people are distributed in a regular pattern.

In another room the people are **clustered**, each person a few centimetres from his nearest neighbour, in small groups with gaps between the groups. This is the science laboratory where pupils are conducting an experiment. There are parts of North Africa where the population is clustered round water supplies.

You may be able to see a room where the distribution is **random**, or haphazard. Which room could that be? And why is the distribution random?

4. Some parts of the school are almost empty. Perhaps the pupils are forbidden to enter these rooms or perhaps they prefer not to go there. You can think of parts of Britain — and other regions of the world — which are empty because they are unpleasant or are 'out of bounds'.

You may already have decided what the various rooms are, simply by observing the distribution of the occupants.

We can see these patterns of population distribution at all scales: fig. 1.5 shows an area of about 50 sq km in which some 50 000 people live, so that the average density of that area must be
50 000 ÷ 50 = 1000 per sq km.
This includes the uninhabited moorland as well as the densely populated town. Most of the 50 000 people are concentrated in the built-up area, the centre of which is near the point at which the tributary joins the main river. From this core,

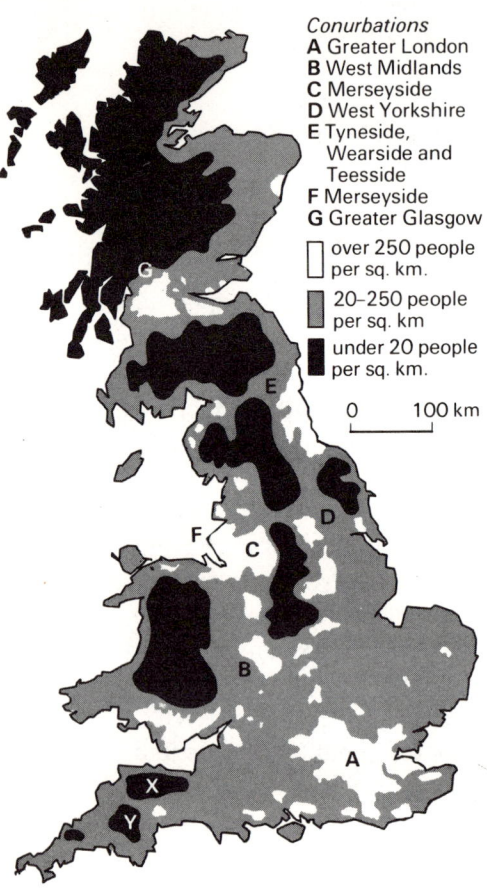

Conurbations
A Greater London
B West Midlands
C Merseyside
D West Yorkshire
E Tyneside,
  Wearside and
  Teesside
F Merseyside
G Greater Glasgow

over 250 people
per sq. km.

20–250 people
per sq. km.

under 20 people
per sq. km.

0   100 km

*figure 1.13 Population distribution:
Great Britain*

Look at fig. 1.14 and suggest
how many people live in each of
A, B and C. Can you match the
photos with the maps and
sketches?

ribbons of settlement extend along the valleys and up the ridges, occasionally swelling into small satellite settlements. These may be old villages engulfed by newer housing. Or they could be recent estates. We can detect the **bridge point** and the **floodplain** and other features which influence the population pattern.

Moving to a larger scale, we could produce a vivid picture of the population pattern of the United Kingdom if we took a picture from the air at night. Such a photo would look like fig. 1.13, showing the large areas of built-up land as white patches, and the sparsely populated areas as patches of black. The two dark patches X and Y in South West England are Dartmoor and Exmoor. There are several large white patches, labelled A to G. These are the **conurbations** which were formed by towns growing so much that they produced one large urban region. This would happen if several towns joined together or if one city grew to absorb the surrounding towns.

Within the urban areas the population density varies. As a matter of fact, those parts of the city which are brightest at night are the very places where hardly anybody lives. It is around the central business districts, in the inner city areas, that the highest densities of 200 per hectare can be found (a hectare is 100 m²). These are often areas of Victorian and Edwardian terraced houses. In the outer suburbs are the large detached houses giving low densities (30 per hectare).

Figure 1.13 shows several large areas of low population density. Even in these thinly peopled areas there are concentrations of population in small towns and villages. We can find these on the AA book maps and on Ordnance Survey maps.

These patterns of distribution are the result of a variety of influences: relief, water supply, soil fertility, communication networks, settlement history, etc. The following ideas are often suggested to answer the question 'what factors determine the distribution of population?'

1. Population densities diminish with increased altitude: the higher the land, the lower the population density.
2. Low population densities tend to be more common in the interiors of continents than on their edges (margins).
3. Flat land is more densely peopled than steeply sloping land.
4. The lower parts of river valleys are usually densely populated.
5. Areas with extremes of temperature and rainfall have low population densities.

SKETCHES

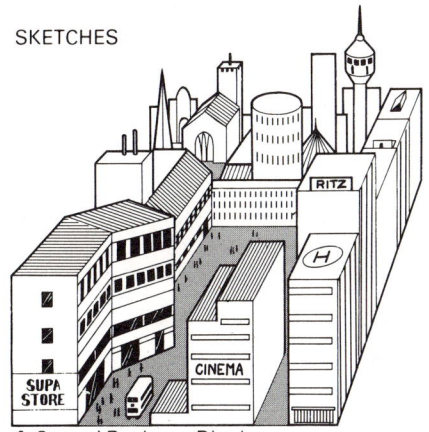

A Central Business District

B Inner city area of Victorian terraced housing mixed with industry

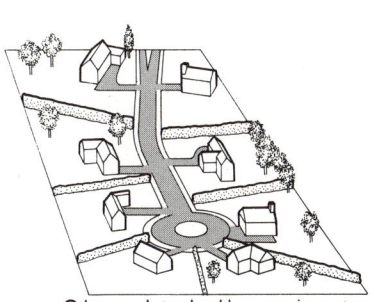

C Large detached houses in outer suburbs

MAPS

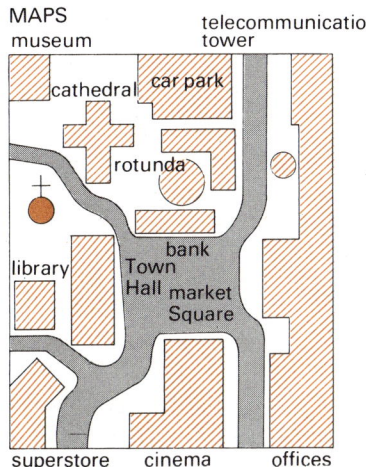

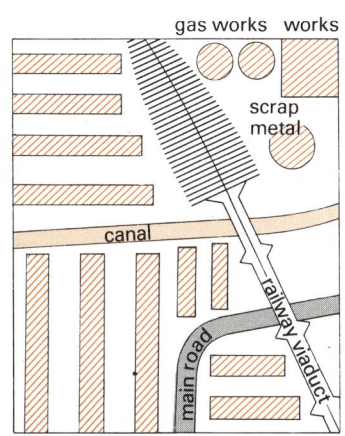

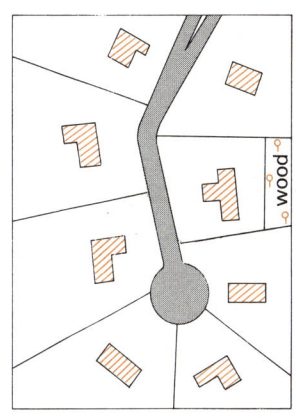

figure 1.14 Variations of population density within cities

6. Tropical areas have high population densities, arctic areas low.
7. Highly industrialised countries have high population densities.
8. In areas where the population is mainly engaged in farming, the density of population is low.

These ideas can be tested by reference to atlases, reference books, various maps and statistics.

If we look more closely at the first hypothesis, at first sight it seems to make sense: highland areas often have cold wet climates, rugged relief, thin soils and poor communication networks. So it seems reasonable to expect them to have fewer people per square kilometre than do the lowland areas. The evidence comes from any atlas: compare a world population map with another showing relief. We can see areas of high land with low population densities (Alps, Rockies, Himalayas, etc.). This supports the hypothesis. But in South America the Andes show higher densities than the nearby coastal lowlands and the Amazon Basin. Similarly, in East Africa there are high population densities at high altitude. So the hypothesis is not acceptable. A new hypothesis might state:

'Population densities generally diminish with altitude in temperate and higher latitudes, but in low latitudes the reverse is usually the case.'

An effective way of testing a hypothesis is by comparing two sets of information (statisticians call them **variables**). Hypothesis 8 above links population density with the percentage of people in agriculture. These two variables are plotted on fig. 1.15. What does the graph tell you about the relationship between population density and the numbers employed in agriculture? How does it alter the hypothesis?

Your maths course may include some statistical methods of measuring correlation. If you have access to a computer you can programme it to produce a correlation index.

figure 1.15 A. **Scattergraph**: *population density and percentage of population employed in agriculture for twenty selected countries B, C, D. Types of statistical correlation*

Does the graph suggest any **correlation** between population density and proportion of population employed in agriculture (hypothesis 8)?

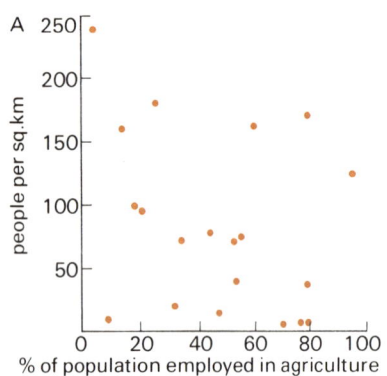

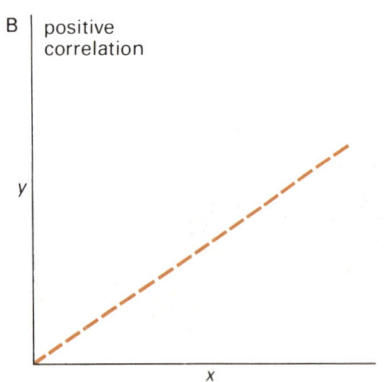

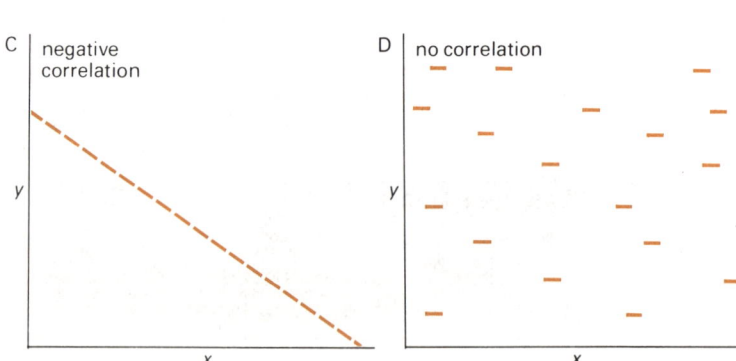

Exercises

1   Draw a simplified version of fig. 1.16.
Show on it the Thames estuary, the low density suburbs, the densely populated city fringe and the low density city centre.

2   (a) Draw a graph to show the change in population density along a line west-east through central London.
Use the statistics and method shown in fig. 1.17.

   (b) Using fig. 1.16 draw a transect north-south through central London. Compare it with the graph for 2(a).

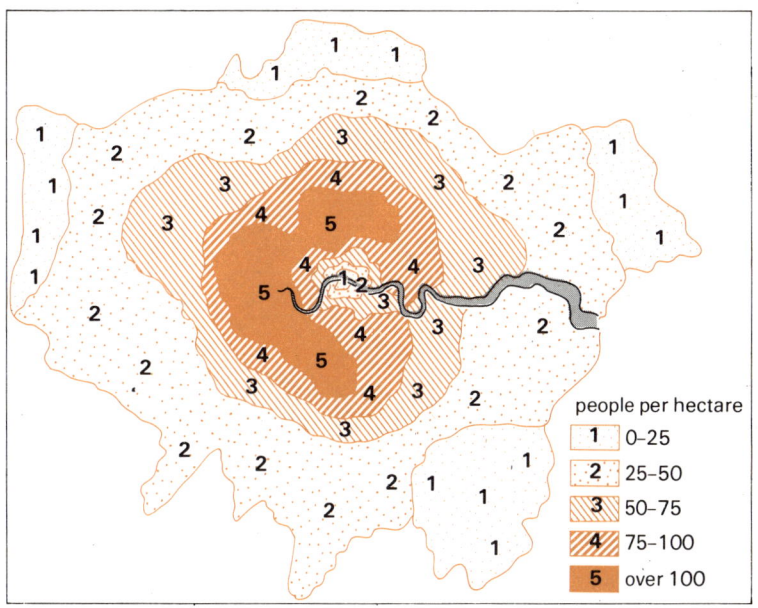

figure 1.16 **Choropleth** *map of population density of London*

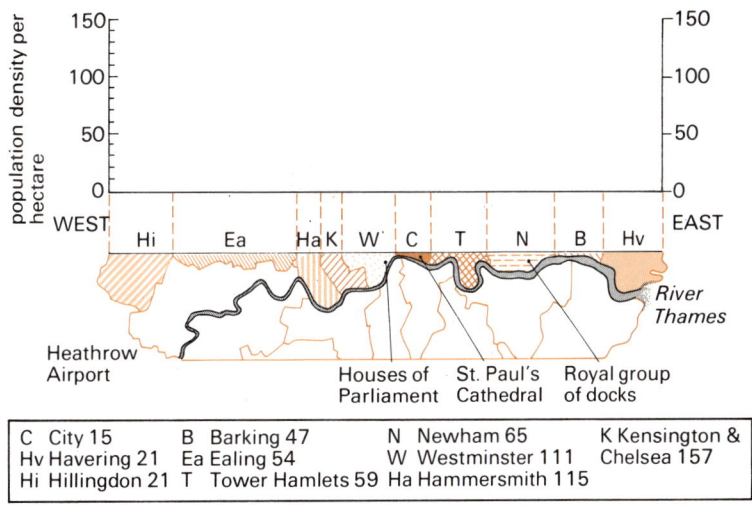

London Boroughs along the line of transect ranked in order of their figures
for population density per hectare

figure 1.17 *West to east population density transect across London*

11

3 (a) Draw a map to show population density in England and Wales.
  Use the information given in fig. 1.18.
  (b) With the help of an atlas offer some reasons for the patterns revealed by the map drawn for 3(a).

4 Examine fig. 1.19 and draw a simplified version of it. Use an atlas to name on it the large sparsely inhabited areas and the areas of dense population.

5 The sketches in fig. 1.14 show features which allow you to recognise the particular part of the city. Make a list of the things you can see which are characteristic of (a) the **CBD** (Central Business District) (b) the inner city area (c) the outer suburbs.

You could add to your list other features known to you, such as modern blocks of flats.

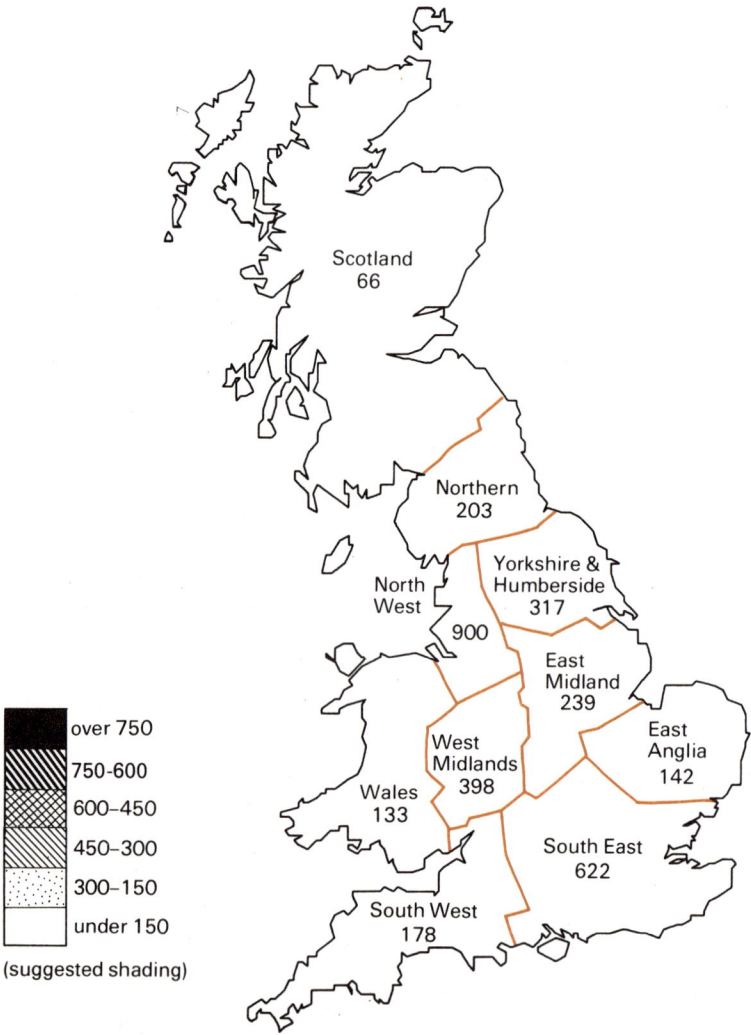

figure 1.18 Average population per square kilometre for the Economic Planning Regions of Great Britain (based on statistics from HMSO Demographic Review *1977)*

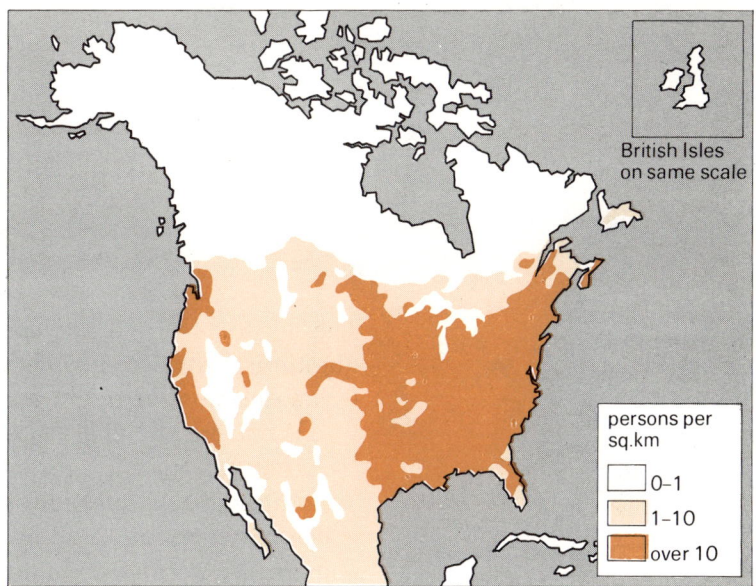

figure 1.19 Population density map of North America

Summary

In this first chapter you have considered a number of important ideas. The check list that follows may help you remember them.

- Big numbers baffle people
- Persuasive statements must be tested
- Diagrams can clarify statistics
- Diagrams can be used to mislead
- Plotting data reveals patterns
- Population patterns repeat at all scales
- Population patterns are ever-changing
- Population patterns can be explained

2 What kinds of people live where?

figure 2.1

The visitor from outer space in fig. 2.1 might ask this question: 'What are people like?'

It is a question we might ask ourselves:

> What are the characteristics which distinguish humans from all other life forms?

To answer this question, we must look for those features which are *common* to all humans (all humans possess them) and are also *peculiar* to humans (only humans possess them). This is part of the study of **anthropology** — 'the science of man'.

The human species (*homo sapiens*) belongs to the order of mammals known as primates. We walk upright on two legs, we can see in three dimensions (stereoscopic vision) and grip with the use of the thumb. We also have large, highly developed brains. But it is our *social organisation*, our *spoken language* and our *technology* which make us different. We can communicate complicated ideas to each other and we can pass knowledge and ideas from one generation to the next. These are the characteristics which distinguish man from the other animals.

Figure 2.2 suggests that early man evolved in the tropical parts of Africa, spreading from there into southern Africa, Asia, Europe and America. Perhaps it was climatic change or the pressure of population which caused early groups of men to migrate to new territory. What is certain is that they encountered new environments and that they developed culturally and physically in response to the change in environment. This process has been called **adaptive radiation**.

The diagram also suggests that the original human populations of America and much of Asia were **mongoloid**; that Central and South Africa were **negroid** and that Europe, North Africa and West Asia were **caucasoid**. These terms are defined on pages 111–12. But this simplified picture of the original distribution of populations — even if it ever existed — was quickly modified by large-scale migrations. For example, many caucasoids moved to colonise South Africa, America and Australasia; many negroids were forcibly moved to the

14

Americas. It is a complex picture but, as we shall see in chapter 4, there is a pattern.

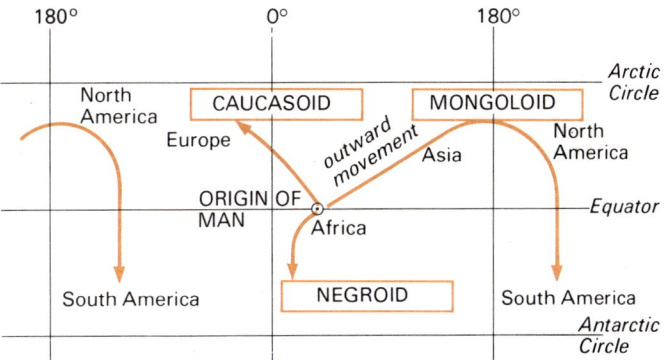

Dispersion is the process of spreading out, in this case early man spreading out over the earth's land surface

figure 2.2 *Adaptive radiation by outward movement from the original home of man in tropical Africa. From common origins, groups adapted over a long period of time to new environments.*

We can start our search for patterns by looking at our own school. Figure 2.3 shows that different sorts of people occupy different parts of the school. Some of the rooms are used by pupils, others by staff. The main difference between those in rooms 1 and 2 is age.

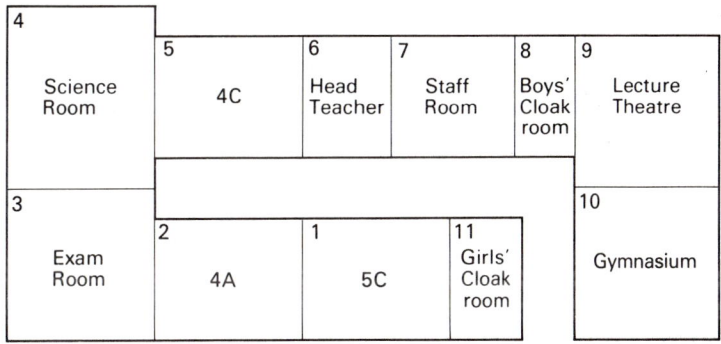

What are the essential differences between the people in these rooms:
    room 6 and room 7
    room 8 and room 11
    room 4 and room 10
    room 2 and room 5?

figure 2.3 *Plan of part of a school building. Different groups of people occupy different parts of this building*

We can see that people in schools are separated according to certain criteria:
    status
    age
    sex
    occupation
    lessons taken
    etc.

You will also notice that the people in your school differ from the people in other schools. You probably attended a nearby school for a lower age group. You will know some schools which are for girls only, some for boys and some mixed. Some schools charge fees and select their pupils, while others are free and unselective. Some schools have a special purpose, such as teaching the blind or the deaf, or teaching music. Some schools are for a certain religion. It may seem as if we go to great trouble and expense to segregate, or split up, pupils of different age, sex, religion, wealth, aptitudes and needs. We certainly make use of labels to indicate what sort of people we can expect to find where. We even put signs on gates, doors or people's blazers:

| STAFF ROOM | FORM 4A |

| INFANTS SCHOOL | GRAMMAR SCHOOL |

| CHURCH OF ENGLAND SCHOOL | etc.

You should ask yourselves what these labels mean. A lot of people do not understand the meaning of the label on their school!

There are usually no labels to help us when we consider the world at a larger scale. But we do notice differences, some of them seeming important, some exaggerated, some irrelevant. And our minds try to make sensible patterns of them: we develop our own mental picture of what sort of people live where. This is part of the **image**, or mental model, which we use to help us understand and respond to the world around us. Our mental models are built from our personal experiences: they are unique, subjective and sometimes imagined. But we can, and should, check our mental model against objectively recorded facts. One of the most useful records is the national **census**.

The census

In the United Kingdom, every ten years, the head of every household is required by law to complete a census form. It asks for details of the members of the household: their age, sex, married status, education, occupation, etc.

All these records are stored in computers from which they can be retrieved as a mass of statistics. Figure 2.4A shows only *one* **population variable** for just one metropolitan

A   Table: Leeds Wards. % of Households Social Class A

Ward 1 8.48	8.01	18.18	9.22	13.16	10.09	43.75
10.34	4.42	28.24	30.50	13.51	6.12	22.22
8.40	22.07	10.94	19.59	8.99	13.54	10.31
3.18	4.41	13.98	23.24	19.18	3.25	12.12
5.19	4.15	34.85	14.91	13.95	14.42	38.36
2.91	25.96	8.07	10.91	15.48	29.03	34.48
25.82	7.01	11.76	15.45	22.56	33.33	31.30
4.23	5.98	6.59	4.40	18.60	29.48	26.09
17.73	6.92	5.17	10.40	15.11	12.50	32.43
2.86	24.96	18.30	16.28	14.95	50.00	25.00
5.55	27.33	8.72	6.29	12.31	30.77	16.67
17.70	4.49	8.57	7.86	8.53	16.67	22.12
5.05	7.29	11.25	11.64	8.70	10.53	31.25
10.53	3.02	5.13	9.04	10.81	20.00	37.50
3.50	8.29	13.64	11.67	12.96	6.09	66.67
					23.21	Ward 106

B

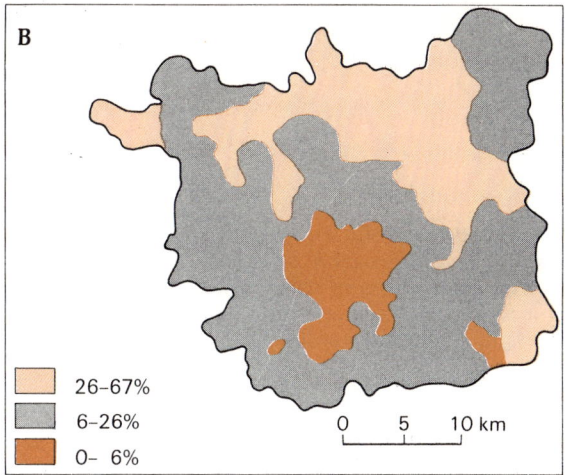

26–67%
6–26%
0–6%

0   5   10 km

figure 2.4 A. Extract from the 1971 census

The point here is that a mass of statistics is not very expressive – it may be very off-putting. But when mapped, the statistics reveal a pattern.

B. Map derived from the 1971 census, showing the percentage of households in the city of Leeds where the head of the house is in Social Class A (defined as 'employers and managers'). A ward is an electoral district.

district. Although the computer has simplified the figures by converting them to percentages, it still looks a formidable mass of numbers. When the figures are plotted as a choropleth map, however, (you constructed a choropleth map in Exercise 3 on p. 12), we see a pattern emerging. The map (fig. 2.4B) allows us to make some generalisations about 'what sort of people live where' in this metropolitan district.

Here are a few generalisations. You may think of others.

1. 'The northern wards have the highest proportion of people in Class A.'
2. 'The upper classes live mostly in the north of the city.'
3. 'The wards with the lowest proportion of people in Class A are in the city centre.'
4. 'The northern suburbs are mostly top class people.' (Note that the map shows the northern wards 'between 26% and 66% Class A', but there is no way of knowing if any of them have more than 50% — unless we look at the original statistics.)
5. 'Only low-class people live in the city centre.'
6. 'People in the higher social classes live in different places from lower class people.'

We can test this statement by making a **scattergraph** (fig. 2.5). This shows that wards with a high percentage of class A always have a low percentage of class D. Even more striking is the coincidence between a high percentage of class D and a low percentage class A.

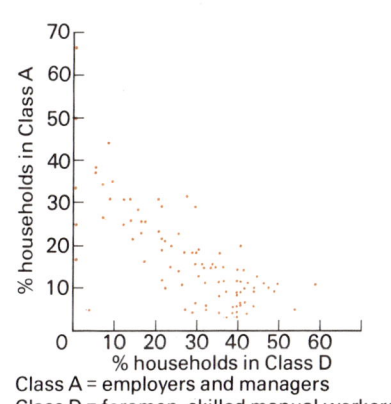

Class A = employers and managers
Class D = foremen, skilled manual workers

figure 2.5 Scattergraph: households in Class A and Class D, 1971, Leeds. Each of the 106 wards is shown by a dot which indicates the percentage of its households in Class A (vertical axis) and Class D (horizontal axis). Apart from the strong clustering, the points all lie close to a line drawn from 45 to 45: a high reading on one axis is accompanied by a low reading on the other. This is a **negative correlation** *– see fig. 1.15, page 10.*

7. 'The upper classes live well away from the city centre.'

See fig. 2.6, which tries to correlate the percentage in class A with distance from the city centre. How does it affect generalisation 7? Can you think of any other method of testing generalisation 7?

NORTH
SOUTH
% households in Class A
40
30
20
10
0
13 12 11 10 9 8 7 6 5 4 3 2 1 0 1 2 3 4 5 6 7 8 9 10
miles from city centre

figure 2.6 Graph showing percentage of Social Class A along a line north to south through Leeds. This north-south transect across the city gives us a **prosperity profile**

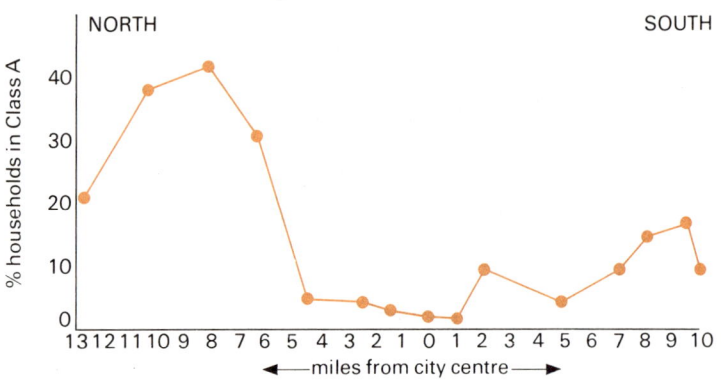

How does fig. 2.7 relate to your own perception of 'what sort of people live where' in a British city? How do maps 1.16 and 2.4 support the idea that the density and type of population varies with distance from the city centre?

RURAL FRINGE
LOW-DENSITY RESIDENTIAL SUBURBS
MEDIUM-DENSITY HOUSING ESTATES
HIGH-DENSITY TERRACED HOUSES
CITY CENTRE
vagrants
manual workers and many old people
skilled manual workers and clerical workers
professional and managerial people
agricultural workers
wealthy satellite dormitory

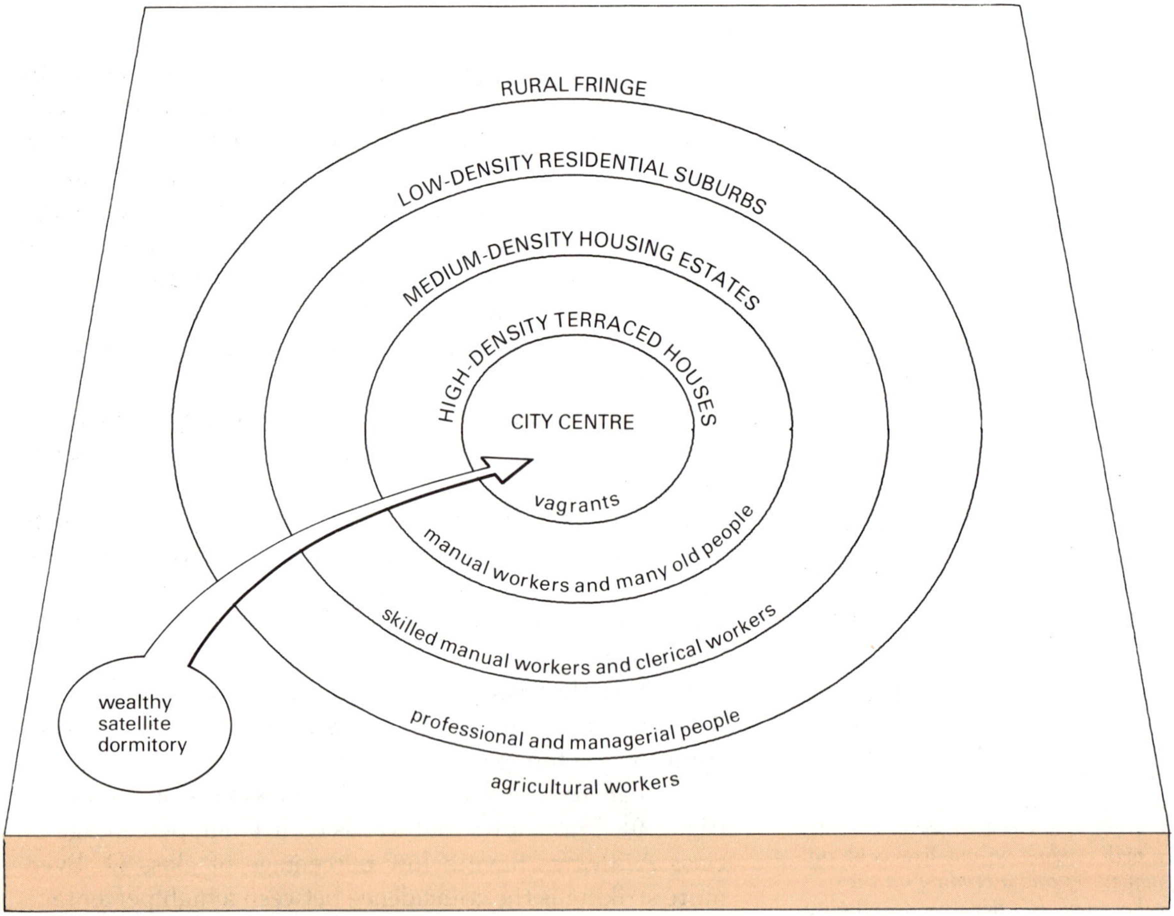

figure 2.7 A simple model of urban housing and socio-economic groups

What sort of people live where in more distant places?

Our mental models are based on first-hand experiences of people and places nearby. When it comes to more distant places we rely on second-hand experiences which we get from comics, magazines, jokes, newspapers, TV, films and books. We get just as much from fiction as from 'documentaries'.

The extract from a comic strip in fig. 2.8 shows German soldiers 'rounding up' Greek peasants. What does it suggest about German soldiers? And about Greek peasants? This is, of course, only a comic. But are you able to test these images against other experiences of Greeks or Germans? If not, the comic may offer you the only ideas you have on the subject. You may decide that it offers unacceptable stereotypes.

A more factual type of information is available to us in the newspapers and on TV. These will be our chief sources of information when we leave school, so we need to know what to expect from them.

The newspapers offer us a lot of ideas about people in distant places. Figure 2.9B uses several 'labels' to tell us about the way people can differ. The 'differentiating characteristics' it mentions are:
'Zulu', suggesting **tribe** and **race**
'Zimbabwe', indicating **nationality**
'President', indicating **rank** in the **hierarchy**
'Headmaster', indicating **occupation** and **rank** and **sex**
'Civil servant', indicating **occupation**
The last two labels suggest **class**.
As usual, **age** is mentioned.

figure 2.8

A

Basque Guerillas Kill Again
From our reporter in Madrid

Following the bomb which killed two Civil Guards, a Basque guerilla leader was shot by unidentified gunmen in St Jean de Luz, a French town near the Spanish border and taken to Bayonne hospital. Identified as Jose Manuel Pagoaga, the seriously wounded ETA separatist leader has sub-machine gun bullet wounds in head and chest.

B

Zulu Chief for President

The post of President of the new Zimbabwe is to be Mr Josiah Zion Gumede, a former headmaster and distinguished civil servant. Mr Gumede, 59, is a descendant of the Zulu kings.

figure 2.9

Summary

In this chapter we have explored the following ideas. You could copy each sentence and make notes under it to remind yourself of examples of each idea.

- The difference between man and other animals is behavioural rather than physiological.
- People differ from each other in many ways.
- Some differences are overstressed.
- People tend to group according to class, religion, occupation, etc.
- The human mind is often too ready to accept stereotypes.
- One of the most important differences between people is their standard of well-being.

19

In the following exercises we consider how people differ and some of the ways in which differences are presented, sometimes exaggerated or distorted.

Exercises

1 *Either* collect some newscuttings about people in distant places,
or use the newspaper cutting in fig. 2.9A.
Use your atlas to find where the places are.
Make a list of all the 'labels' used (e.g. 'Basque', 'Guerilla')
Beside each label note (a) what it means (b) what characteristic it refers to (e.g. nationality, religion).
Are the news items factual and fair, or do they seem to emphasise things which are sensational or horrific?
Indicate any words which are emotive or which may show bias.

2 The following quotation is from a Geography book.
'The Japanese are short and wiry because of the hard struggle on overpopulated islands.'
(a) Imagine you are Japanese. Write a brief note to the author of that quotation, commenting on what it says.
(b) If you are not Japanese, write a letter to a penfriend in Japan, politely asking the sort of questions which will allow you to decide if the statements in the quotation are true.

3 This quotation might be comical if it was not also very offensive.
'The people of the hot lands can, as a rule, obtain the things they need with comparatively little effort: in many respects their life is too easy, and so they are apt to be slothful and unenterprising.'
Make a list of the generalisations you would like to test. How would you try to find out what the author meant by 'hot', 'things they need', 'little effort', 'easy', 'slothful'?

A

Ward no.	% residents born in New Commonwealth	Ward no.	% residents born in New Commonwealth	Ward no.	% residents born in New Commonwealth
1	0.89	36	0.30	71	0.37
2	0.48	37	0.55	72	0.02
3	0.42	38	0.16	73	0.12
4	1.25	39	0.06	74	0.12
5	0.64	40	0.52	75	0.38
6	2.29	41	0.20	76	0.29
7	0.94	42	0.24	77	0.03
8	7.12	43	0.12	78	0.17
9	0.40	44	0.12	79	0.28
10	0.83	45	0.11	80	0.36
11	0.67	46	0.10	81	0.51
12	0.39	47	0.32	82	0.00
13	17.82	48	0.91	83	0.27
14	4.76	49	0.51	84	0.17
15	2.36	50	0.15	85	0.00
16	0.44	51	0.07	86	0.00
17	0.24	52	0.34	87	0.00
18	0.50	53	1.50	88	0.37
19	0.71	54	0.06	89	0.00
20	0.52	55	0.28	90	0.32
21	3.36	56	0.44	91	0.16
22	0.48	57	0.07	92	0.46
23	17.03	58	0.04	93	0.39
24	0.28	59	0.54	94	0.43
25	0.74	60	0.16	95	0.22
26	1.09	61	1.23	96	1.22
27	5.44	62	0.52	97	0.87
28	0.54	63	0.17	98	0.31
29	8.15	64	0.26	99	0.35
30	0.45	65	0.29	100	0.51
31	0.17	66	0.14	101	0.00
32	0.80	67	0.16	102	0.52
33	0.23	68	0.46	103	0.00
34	0.28	69	0.23	104	0.39
35	0.75	70	0.50	105	2.22
				106	0.06

figure 2.10 Leeds: percentage of residents who were born in the New Commonwealth (derived from the 1971 census)

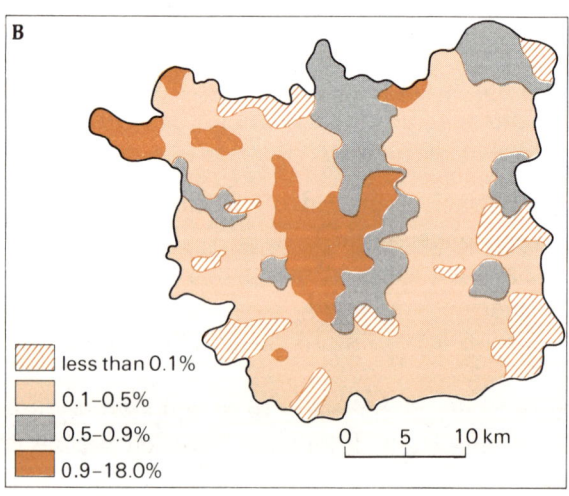

B

less than 0.1%
0.1–0.5%
0.5–0.9%
0.9–18.0%

0   5   10 km

4 Write a paragraph to summarise the characteristics which distinguish *homo sapiens* from all other species. You may use information from this chapter and from the library.

5 Describe the pattern revealed by the map in fig. 2.10. Now plot the statistics on a dispersion diagram (see fig. 1.2 to find out how to construct a dispersion diagram). Make the vertical scale 0% to 100%. Does this alter the impression you get from the map?

6 Make a copy of fig. 2.7. Show on your diagram where the house adverts listed below would best fit.

COMPACT STONE BUILT TERRACE HOUSE

EMINENTLY SUITABLE FOR
FIRST TIME BUYER

116 PARKSIDE STREET, WILBERTON. Handily placed on a quiet street within easy reach of town centre, the property comprises: living room with built in cupboards and fitted gas fire in modern tiled surround, small kitchenette, double bedroom and bathroom with three piece suite. **PRICE £5250.** View by key.

COUNTRY COTTAGE

27 MOON TERRACE, OXLIP. Truly rural cottage nestled in a small row of similar properties in this quiet backwater. Offering three bedroomed, centrally heated accommodation away from the bustle of town and city yet still within easy commuting distance of major industrial centres. 18 ft lounge. Kitchen/dining room. Three bedrooms. Bathroom with 3 piece suite in white. Small yard to rear and medium sized cottage garden to front. **Price £17,950.** View via agents.

NAYLOR AVENUE, BURTON – £16,500

Excellent BAY WINDOWED SEMI ideally situated just off the main road, standing in medium sized gardens with 17 ft garage. Hall with cloaks, through lounge/dining area, kitchen, 3 bedrooms, bathroom/w.c. in pink.

MODERNISED TERRACE OFF VICARAGE STREET

Conveniently situated, this property is in good decorative order, and has the benefit of modern window frames and enjoys an open aspect to both front and rear. Comprises: Sitting room with gas fire in 'Tudor Stone' fireplace, dining kitchen with gas fire, basement, two bedrooms, bathroom, attic bedroom, yard to rear. R.V.£58. **Price £7950.**

CHARLESVILLE STREET

A very pleasant through terrace house, situated in a popular residential community. This delightful property has the benefit of a GARDEN, and is offered at a modest price to allow for some minor modernisation. Comprises: Sitting room, living kitchen, fitted gas fire, basement, two bedrooms, bathroom with pink suite, attic/occasional bedroom. R.V.£65. **Price £6950**

40 LONGFELLOW STREET, WILBERTON

A modern detached house in a first class residential area. Fully redecorated throughout and refurbished with new bathroom suite and kitchen units. Lounge, kitchen, 4 bedrooms, bathroom, separate w.c. Full gas fired central heating. Good sized gardens front and rear. Integral garage. **Price £29,950.** View via agents.

PANORAMIC OUTLOOK, THREE BEDROOMED DETACHED BUNGALOW

OAKHEATH. In an isolated convenient position, beautiful outlook across valley, larger than average accommodation, full central heating. Vestibule; hall; 19 ft lounge, gas fire in fireplace, spot lights, Cornish slate hearth, built-on boiler house; dining kitchen with fitted breakfast bar, twin stainless steel sink bowls, auto plumbing. Three bedrooms, all fully fitted; bathroom/w.c., separate shower cubicle. Garden and patio. Detached garage, caravan parking, ample further space for cars. **£32,500.**

SUPERBLY APPOINTED DETACHED RESIDENCE

Individually designed, stone faced DETACHED RESIDENCE, occupying a large plot at the head of a quiet cul-de-sac. The property has GAS CENTRAL HEATING, and integral garage, car port and ample parking space for numerous vehicles. Comprises: Entrance hall, cloakroom, dining room, with open archway to recreation room/secondary lounge, with built-in storage units, kitchen with superb range of fitted units, utility room, bedroom, on the first floor, principal lounge with French windows on to balcony, master bedroom with fitted wardrobes, further bedroom, spacious bathroom with avocado suite. Attractive gardens. R.V.£352. **Price £44,500.**

BAGLEY CRESCENT, CHILLINGFORD –£18,500

Superbly decorated SEMI DETACHED BUNGALOW with EXPENSIVE FIXTURES AND FITTINGS including SEALED UNIT DOUBLE GLAZING and an INSTANT GAS WATER HEATER. Hall, superb lounge, fully fitted dining kitchen. 2 good bedrooms, one with built in furniture, bathroom/w.c. Neat gardens with PERMANENT GARAGE.

VICTORIAN TERRACED HOUSE PROVIDING FOUR BEDSIT ACCOMMODATION – IDEAL INVESTMENT – ALTERNATIVELY COULD BE RECONVERTED BACK TO PROVIDE FAMILY ACCOMMODATION

302 LONDON ROAD, OXLEY. Full gas fired central heating, in pleasant decorative condition. Entrance hall; lounge with gas fire; fitted kitchen with sink unit, extractor fan. In the basement: Dining room/TV room; kitchen. On the first floor: Two further rooms; bathroom with white suite; overall attic self-contained room, ideal for youth wing or granny flat, dormer window, wall lights. Separate shower cubicle and kitchen area. **£13,950.** View by key.

END LANE FARM COTTAGE

A most attractive stone built End Terraced Cottage situated in this enviable position overlooking open countryside. Entrance porch with store off, dining kitchen, 18 ft 6 in lounge, 2 bedrooms, bathroom. Attractive cottage garden, space for garage. In need of some modernisation. The property is offered at the very realistic price of **£13,950.**

Test the model in fig. 2.7 by collecting some 'for sale' adverts for houses in your home town. Arrange them on a town map and then compare the result with fig. 2.7. Can you explain any differences between the two maps?

7 Obtain the 1981 census data for your home region (your teacher may be able to get them for you from the local planning department) and produce your own social class maps and graphs like figs. 2.4 and 2.5 for your home region. What sort of pattern emerges? Is it the pattern you had expected? Is it like the patterns in figs. 2.4 and 2.5?

3 Population dynamics

figure 3.1 A matter of life and death

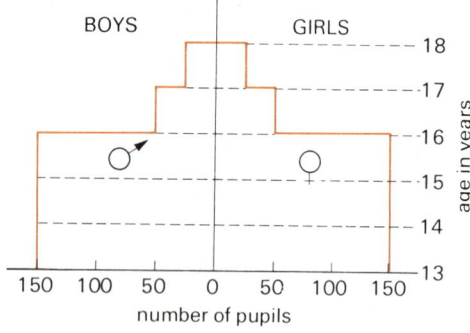

figure 3.2 A **population pyramid** showing the age/sex structure of a typical school population

The school referred to in fig. 3.2 has 150 girls and 150 boys entering each year at age 13. Each year 200 pupils leave at age 16, 50 leave at age 17, and 50 leave at age 18. So there is a balance between 'arrivals' and 'departures'. The school's population stays at 1050.

But next year there will be only 250 entrants. And in the following four years we expect only 200 per year. Can you predict the size of the school's population in five years' time?

This is a simple small-scale example of a fluctuating population. It shows pupils in year groups moving through the school and so it may help you to think of population as *a flow of people through time*. It suggests why we need to predict **population change**.

The supply of books, classroom space, use of fuel, equipment and foodstuffs, even the numbers of teachers required and the types of lesson which can be offered, are all affected by the size of the school population.

We shall see that at larger scales beyond the school it is important to consider how the availability of space, energy, food supplies and other resources will be affected by population change.

A matter of life and death

Table 3.1 shows the number of births and deaths per year in an English city during the decade 1961–71.

It shows births steady at about 8000 a year and the death rate fairly stable at around 6000 a year. This gap between births and deaths is the **natural change** — in this case an *increase* of some 2000 a year. What was the natural change during 1970?

A 'changing volume' model

The relationship between births and deaths is often illustrated by a 'bathtub analogy'. See fig. 3.3A.

If the flow into the bath exceeds the outflow, the level in

table 3.1   *Births and deaths in Bradford 1961–71*

Year	Births	Deaths	Natural change
1961	8097	6216	
1962	8418	6398	
1963	8489	6432	
1964	8667	5952	
1965	8452	6257	
1966	8283	6530	
1967	8257	5945	
1968	8177	6334	
1969	8242	6319	
1970	8367	6107	
1971	8210	5961	

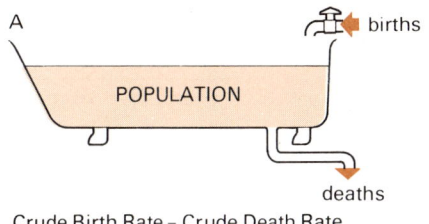

Crude Birth Rate – Crude Death Rate
= Natural Change

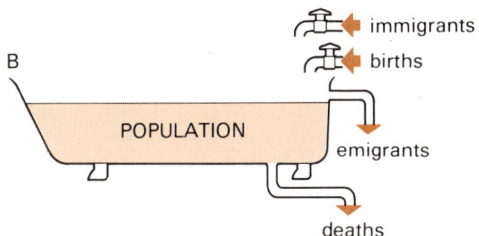

(**Births** + Immigration) – (Deaths + Emigration)
= Population Change

figure 3.3 A. Bathtub analogy to illustrate effect of births and deaths on population change
B. Bathtub analogy extended

the bath should increase, and vice-versa. This can be shown by a simple formula:

CRUDE BIRTH RATE minus CRUDE DEATH RATE equals NATURAL CHANGE

$$CBR - CDR = NC$$

We can test this with some figures:

In 1961 the population of Calderdale, West Yorkshire, was	201 165
The natural change (CBR − CDR) 1961–71 was an increase of	+4 910
which should have given a 1971 population of	206 075
But the population of Calderdale in 1971 was in fact	195 189

So there seems to have been a 'leak' from Calderdale of 10 886

Clearly, this 'leak' of 10 886 people can be explained only by the movement of people out of Calderdale to live elsewhere. We have to add to the 'bathtub' diagram another 'tap' for arrivals and another 'outlet' for departures, as in fig. 3.3B. Can you see why the 'bathtub' model may now be unacceptable? It does, however, show us this equation:

(births + **immigration**) − (deaths + **emigration**)
= population change

The population change in Great Britain since World War II is shown in table 3.2.

Note that **natural change** is the balance between births and deaths

and **net migration** is the balance between immigration and emigration.

table 3.2   Population change in Great Britain (thousands)

Years	1946–51	1951–56	1956–61	1961–66	1966–71	1971–72	1972–73	1973–74
Natural change	300	200	261	338	276	188	124	77
Net migration	−38	−35	+43	−8	−75	−20	+16	−44
Total change	262	165	304	330	201	168	140	33

There is a great deal more natural change than migration, but the gap is narrowing. Some people may be surprised to find that there is an almost continual loss by migration.

The formulae we have been using can be applied to any country or region. They apply equally to animal populations. But when we come to world population totals we can ignore migration. Is this still true and likely to remain so?

The graph of world population growth (fig. 3.4) shows that for thousands of years the population, despite some fluctuations, was growing steadily. Then in the eighteenth century came a rapid increase, the 'population explosion'. It is shown very dramatically in fig. 3.5. This graph appears on the cover of an Open University booklet. Why does it look so different from fig. 3.4? The vertical axis shows years. The horizontal axis shows population totals, with zero in the centre so as to give two symmetrical curves: the total is plotted in two equal halves on each side of zero. Why have

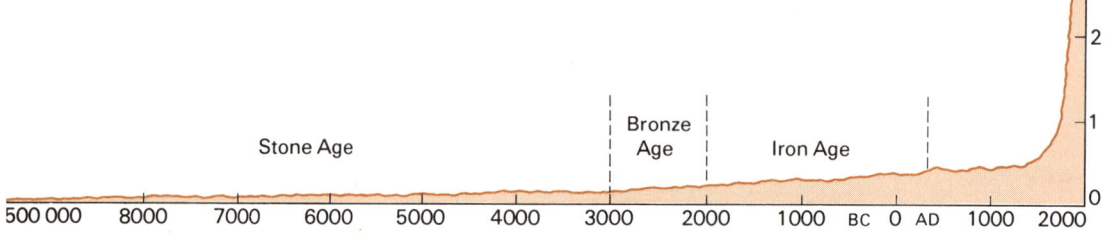

figure 3.4 World population growth

they made such a graph? It carries a clear message. And the cartoon which appears on the same book cover (fig. 3.6) suggests not only an explosion but also the causes and consequences of that explosion. You should ask yourself what the cartoon says to you. When linked with the graph, does it seem convincing? Remember, you should think carefully before you accept ideas which are presented in a very persuasive form.

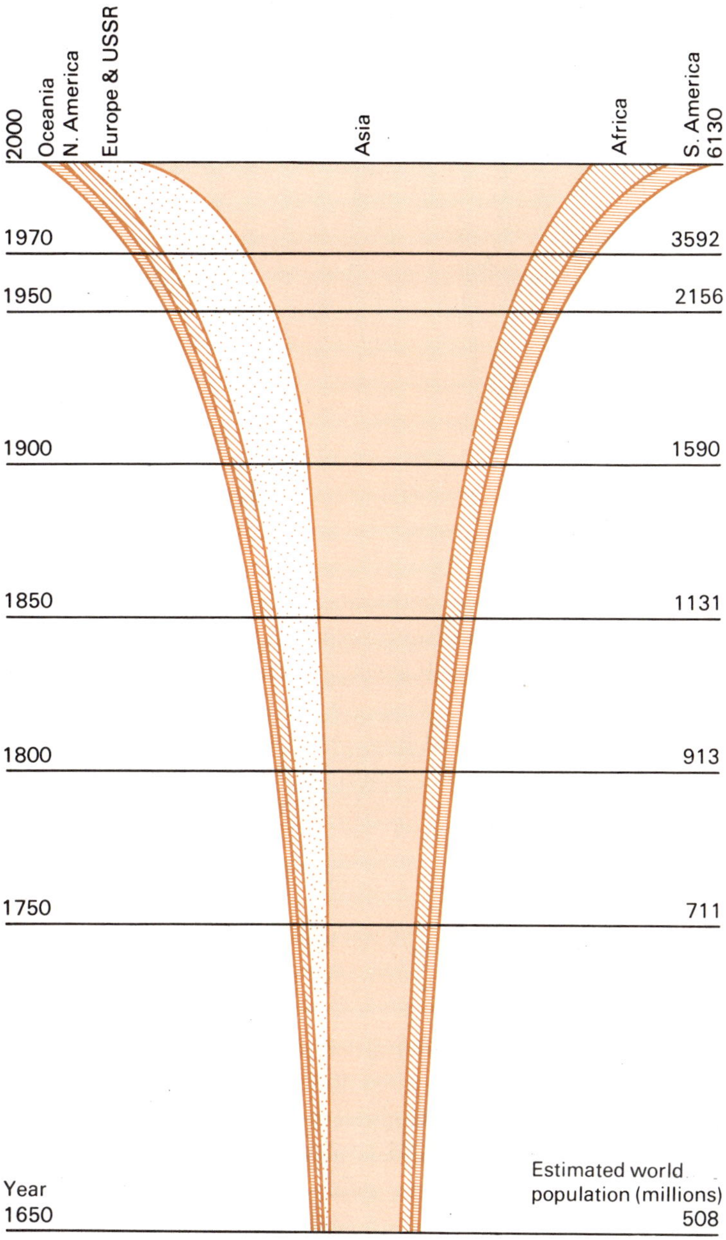

Oceania
N. America
Europe & USSR
2000

Asia

Africa

S. America
6130

1970 ——————————————————— 3592

1950 ——————————————————— 2156

1900 ——————————————————— 1590

1850 ——————————————————— 1131

1800 ——————————————————— 913

1750 ——————————————————— 711

Year
1650

Estimated world
population (millions)
508

figure 3.5 World population change

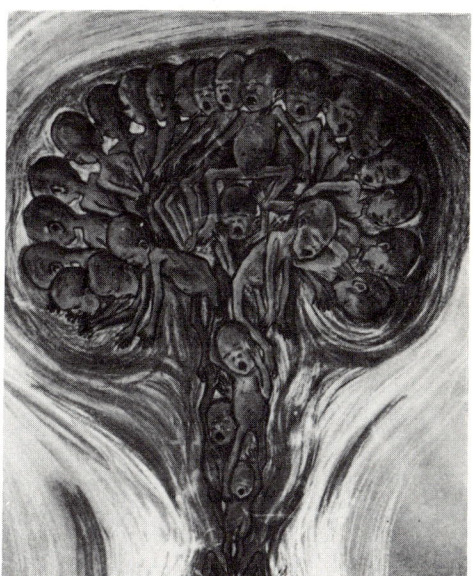

figure 3.6 The population explosion

How many of us will there be?

This is one of the most important questions we can ask ourselves. Unfortunately, all we can say with certainty about population prediction is that it is uncertain. The **demographers** (people who study population) have never got it right yet. The reason is that there are so many **variables** affecting population growth. Figure 3.7 tries to summarise

figure 3.7 *Some of the factors which affect fertility rates in prosperous nations*

some of the factors which affect **fertility** rates in the prosperous countries of the world.

1. Women have career alternatives to childbearing
2. Children can be a financial liability
3. It is a long time — if ever — before children are a source of income
4. People marry later in life
5. They have financial commitments in early marriage (e.g. mortgage and HP) which delay childbearing
6. They can enjoy an attractive lifestyle (e.g. second car, winter skiing) and may see children as a threat to it
7. They have easy access to efficient contraception
8. Uncertain employment prospects

For all these reasons there has been a decline in the fertility rates of all prosperous nations. In West Germany a survey tried to find how many children the adults intended to produce. Between 1974 and 1976 the number of people intending to have only *one* child increased five-fold. The number of people wanting *no children* doubled in the same period. This is just one reason for the West German government forecast that the population of the country would drop by a third over the next fifty years. So the government suggested incentives, e.g. to pay over £200 a month for six months after the birth of a baby. The Chancellor at the time, Helmut Schmidt, rejected these proposed incentives, saying, 'I am convinced that the happiness of a nation does not lie in having more births than deaths'.

At the same time the Chinese government was introducing financial *disincentives* to childbearing. Couples who had more than one child would have their income reduced. And in India the Prime Minister's son fell from power because of his compulsory sterilisation campaign. Keep an eye open for news items telling of similar measures by governments attempting to influence population growth.

Patterns of change

We have seen how the change in size of a population can be graphed and mapped. Now we look at the methods of showing how the population is changing in composition or 'make-up'.

Figure 3.8 represents a family of six, giving the age and sex of each individual. If we add to this a sample of neighbours we can produce an age/sex profile of their neighbourhood. This can be plotted on a graph to produce a **population pyramid**. The pyramid in fig. 3.9 represents a neighbourhood on an inter-war housing estate with mostly grown-up families: the under-ten and the over-sixty age groups are fairly small. A newer estate would have younger parents and children. The pyramid will look very different when the present teenagers have gone.

Pyramids for such small areas may be distorted by local features — they differ from regional or national pyramids. You can see how the pyramid for Headingley (a suburb of Leeds) differs from the total Leeds pyramid (fig. 3.10). Can you think of any reasons for these differences? What can the pyramids tell the Planning Department about the community's needs for amenities such as day nurseries or Senior Citizen Centres?

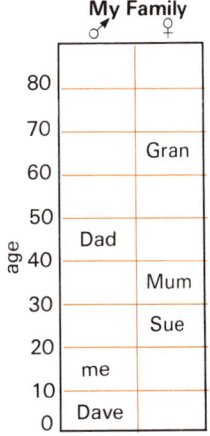

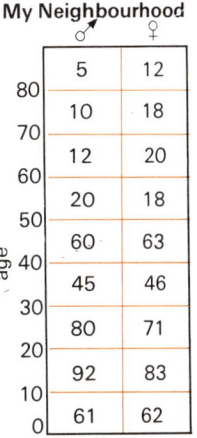

figure 3.8 Family and neighbourhood age/sex patterns

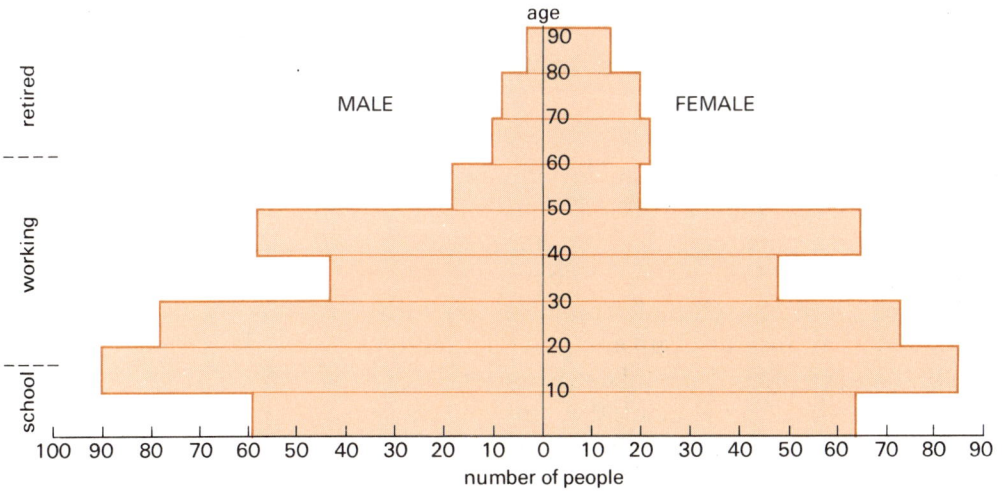

figure 3.9 Population pyramid for a neighbourhood

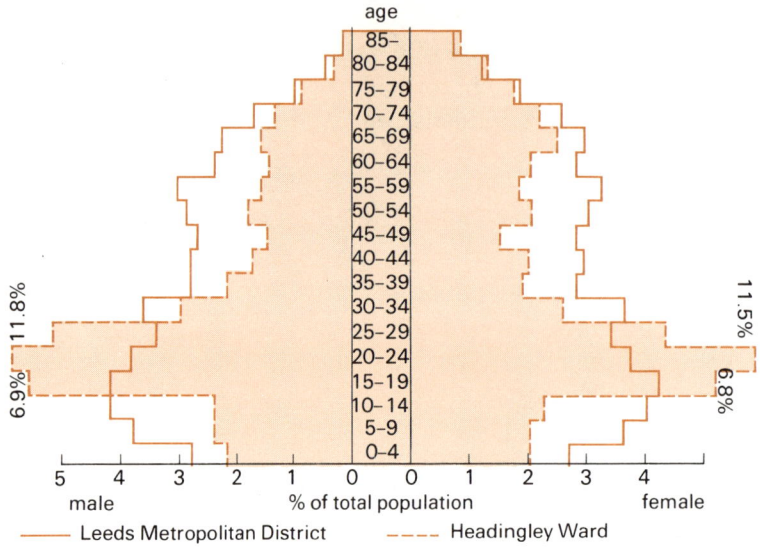

figure 3.10 Population pyramid for Ward 13, Headingley, and for the whole of Leeds Metropolitan District, 1978

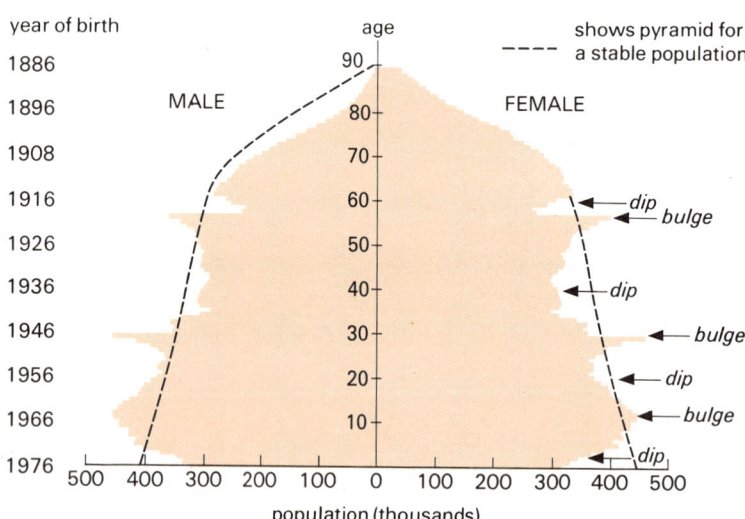

figure 3.11 Population pyramid for Great Britain, 1976

The pyramid for Great Britain shows many fluctuations but, perhaps surprisingly, the number of males and females born in a given year (the population **cohort**) is almost equal. We can see the pyramid shrinking steadily above age 60. Above this age, which shrinks faster, male or female? We see 'shrinkages' or 'dips' in the upper 50 group and around 35 and in the lower 20s but, most striking, a shrinkage below age 10. When were the 'bulges' born? Can you link the 'dips' and the 'bulges' with any well-known historical events or periods? Figure 3.11 shows with a dotted line the shape of a pyramid for a stable or slowly growing population.

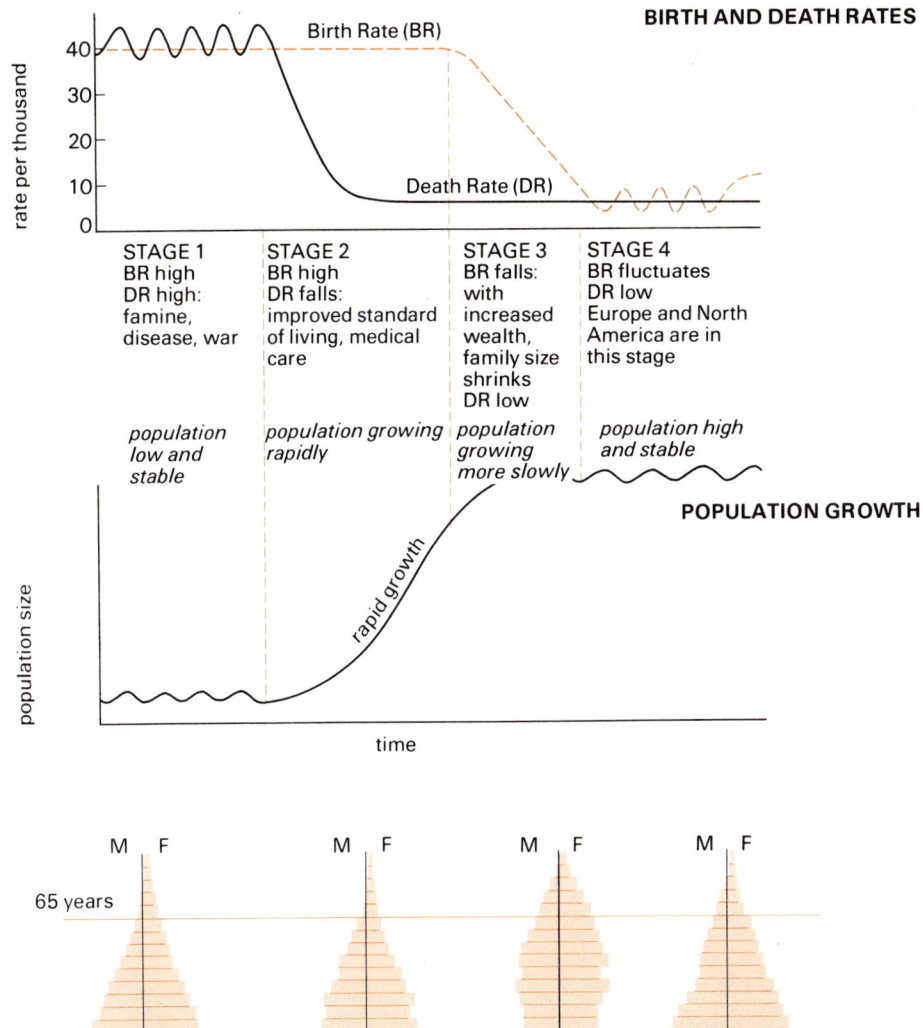

figure 3.12 Demographic transition: changes in birth rate and death rate

Another way of analysing changes in a country's population is to plot on the same graph both the birth rate and the death rate for a given period. This has been done for an imaginary country in fig. 3.12. When birth rate (BR) and death rate (DR) coincide, there is no change. When the birth rate is above the death rate there is a natural increase. Notice that at first the country had a high birth rate and a high but fluctuating death rate, from famine, war and disease. As standards of health, hygiene and medical care improved, the death rate dropped sharply but births remained high: there was a big *natural increase* in population. Then, with increas-

Note that there are several computer programs on the market which allow you to experiment with population statistics

ing wealth, education and technology, the birth rate fell to the level of death rates. Now, although the birth rate fluctuates slightly, the population is fairly stable. Demographers suggest that as countries develop they pass through the four stages of **demographic transition** shown in fig. 3.12. The rich countries of the world have gone through all these stages. But most countries are still in stage 2, with rapidly growing populations. In a few countries, the birth rate is falling below the death rate.

Balance and control

We saw in fig. 3.4 the rate at which the earth's population is growing. You should by now be thinking of a 1980 world population of over 4 billion (4 000 000 000), with a birth rate around 30 per thousand and a death rate near 12 per thousand, giving an annual increase of 18 per thousand (nearly 2 per cent). This will result in an extra 2 billion people on the earth before the end of the twentieth century. But we have already reached the stage where many countries have an average intake of food below the minimum for normal health. This gives rise to problems like those suggested by fig. 3.13, and the important question of how to balance population and food supply.

Population theory in the past has stressed that the growth of population is geometric (1 to 2, to 4, to 8 . . .) whereas food supply can only increase arithmetically (1 to 2, to 3, to 4 . . .). This idea was at the core of a famous 'Essay on the Principles of Population' by a parson named Thomas Malthus in 1798. He predicted that population would always grow beyond the point where food supply could support it. We can express this idea as a graph (fig. 3.14).

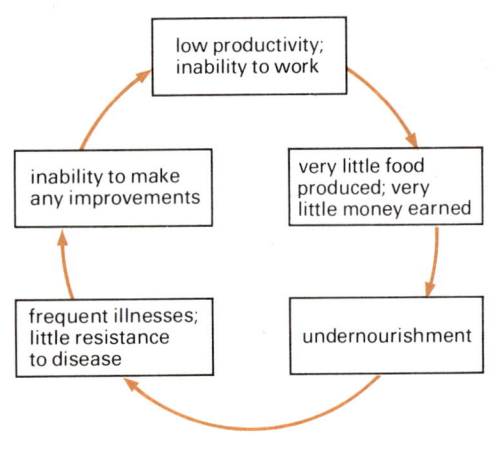

figure 3.13 The poverty cycle

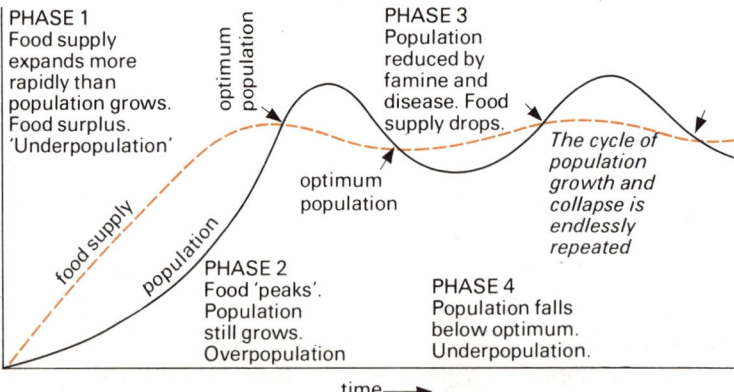

figure 3.14 Graph to illustrate the ideas of Malthus

This simple but pessimistic idea gave rise to a widespread philosophy of gloom and despair: mankind is seen as the prisoner of harsh natural laws from which there is no escape. But you will be able to think of some very important considerations which the Rev. Malthus overlooked or could not have predicted:

1. *Cheap and easily available contraception* Malthus advocated delayed marriage but no restriction of child-bearing once married.
2. *The technological revolution* Some countries have improved their agricultural methods so much as to produce huge, and often embarrassing, surpluses of foods, especially grains, meat and dairy produce. We shall discuss this **green revolution** later.
3. *Improved communications* These make it possible to redistribute the earth's food supplies and to spread the knowledge of 1 and 2.

Summary

In this chapter we have considered the following ideas:

- Population size and composition fluctuates
- Predicting population change is almost impossible
- Variations in size and composition can be graphed and mapped, revealing patterns
- Some governments try to influence population change
- Population change = births − deaths
- Population change is influenced by a lot of factors such as
    economic prosperity
    social attitudes
    medical knowledge
- Population is a flow of people through time

The exercises which follow will illustrate some of the ideas presented in this chapter.

Exercises

1 Use the method shown in figs 3.8 and 3.9 to produce a population pyramid for your own neighbourhood or the school catchment.
NB. Do not ask your neighbours delicate questions about their age — make an estimate.
Write a report on the result of the exercise, relating the shape of the pyramid to the type of neighbourhood and the services provided for it (amenity provision). When you have finished, write a criticism of the method you have used.

2 Draw a simple 'bathtub' analogy diagram to illustrate the factors influencing population growth. Then draw a 'bathtub' to illustrate the figures for *either* your home region *or* Calderdale (page 23).

3 Draw a graph to show the growth of world population. Print on your diagram some notes to highlight and explain the main features of the graph.

4 Draw a 'cartoon' which is a version of fig. 3.7 for a poor country.
Write some comments on the difference between attitudes to child-bearing in prosperous nations and in poor countries.

5 Look at fig. 3.12. Explain how the population pyramids below the graphs relate to the stages of 'demographic transition'.

6 Produce a simple version of fig 3.15, showing the population structure of Botswana. Print on it your comments, especially on the number of males aged 20 to 40. Does the pyramid suggest which stage Botswana has reached on the 'transition' model?

7 Figure 3.13 shows how a diagram can be used to demonstrate how events and situations are linked. Experiment with drawing similar diagrams to show Malthus' ideas (fig. 3.14).

8 Use the statistics in table 3.1 to draw a graph showing 'natural population change in a British city'. Describe the result.

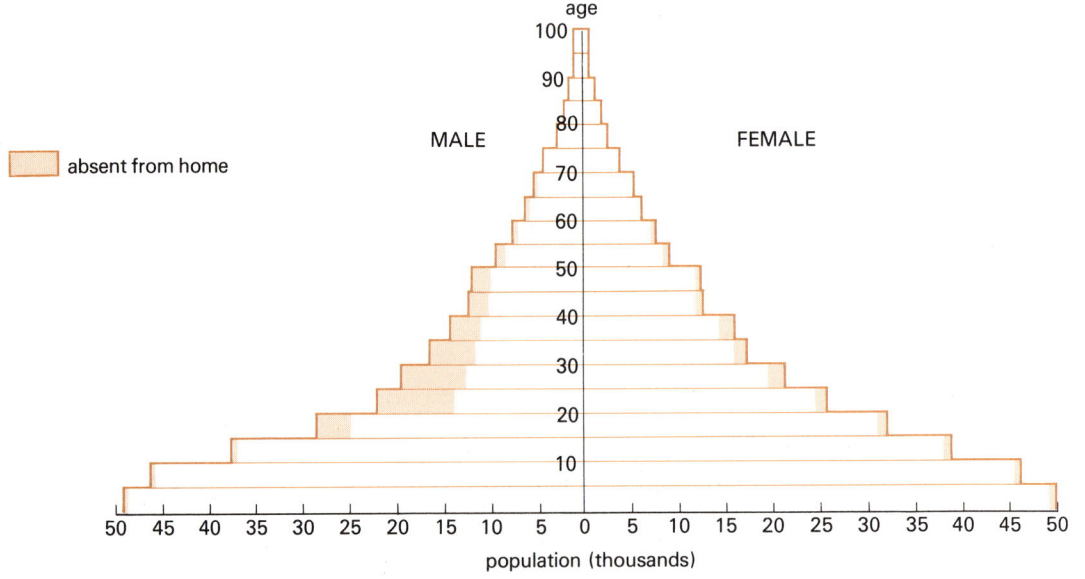

figure 3.15 Population pyramid for Botswana, 1971 (based on Republic of Botswana, Report on the Population Census 1971)

4 People on the move

And now you live dispersed on ribbon roads,
And no man knows or cares who is his neighbour
Unless his neighbour makes too much disturbance,
But all dash to and fro in motor cars,
Familiar with the roads and settled nowhere.

T. S. Eliot *Choruses from 'The Rock'*

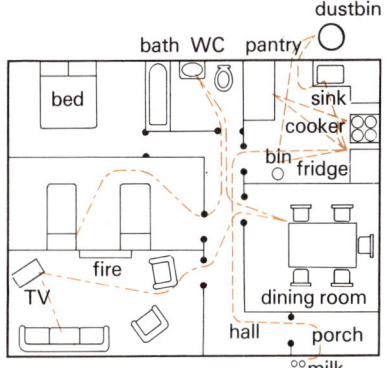

figure 4.1 Humans moving around the house

Draw a plan like fig. 4.1 to show your movements around the house during a typical weekday

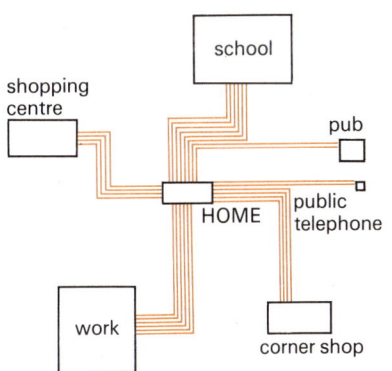

figure 4.2 Journeys around town. Each line represents one journey. The size of each box indicates the length of stay

Moving around the house

Some of the satellites which orbit the earth are equipped with sensors capable of detecting people moving around on the ground below. Imagine one of these was beamed down on your house for a day and the resulting 'picture' came to you for analysis. See fig. 4.1.

If you analyse the flow lines you will see patterns. On each journey you move to a part of the house where something is available which you need or want at a particular time of day: food, water, heat, entertainment, sleep, etc. When you need something which is not stored, piped in or delivered, you have to make a journey outside the house.

Journeys round town

In fig. 4.2 the width of the lines indicates the number of journeys each week; the size of the 'destination' indicates the length of stay (e.g. the thin line to the phone booth shows one journey, the tiny box shows you didn't stay long). These journeys are all short-distance and short-stay, but frequent. They show up on fig. 4.3 in a pattern very similar to the daily fluctuations of air temperature. We can see in fig. 4.3 a **diurnal** (daily) **rhythm** of brief, but frequent, journeys.

Some of the things we need or desire can only be reached by long and less frequent excursions. **Annual**, or once-a-year, trips are shown in fig. 4.4. As it happens, these are for pleasure. But some people make seasonal movements over large distances in search of work, some in search of water or pasture for their animals.

33

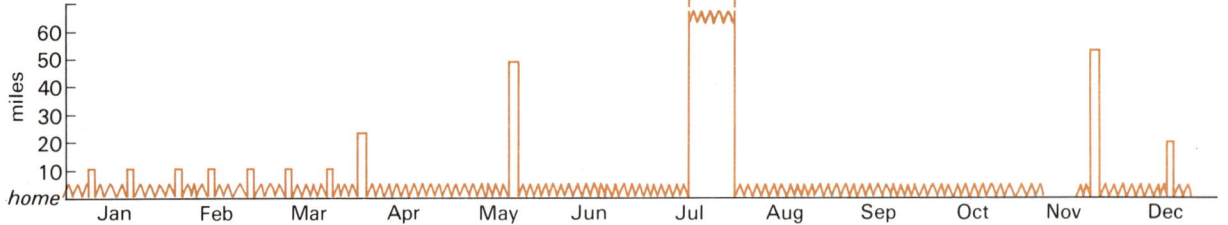

figure 4.3 Graph of a British school pupil's journeys for a year (much simplified because of space)

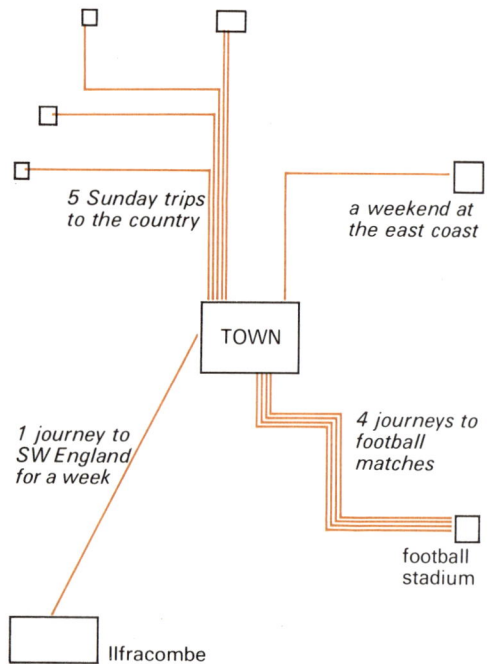

5 Sunday trips
to the country

a weekend at
the east coast

TOWN

1 journey to
SW England
for a week

4 journeys to
football
matches

football
stadium

Ilfracombe

figure 4.4 Excursions over a year

Patterns of movement

The most common movement of human beings is the daily journey from home to the fields, the factory, the office or to school, returning home in the evening. Most of us spend our lives in this simple rhythm. We move over a space which is familiar to us and we come to think of it as our 'territory'. We develop a strong attachment to it, even if it is in reality inhospitable (like the fringe of a desert) or positively dangerous (like the slopes of a volcano or the banks of a treacherous river). There has to be a strong attraction from another territory, or something very repellent in our own, to persuade us to move our home. But many of us do move our homes for long periods, even permanently. It is then that we speak of **migration**: long-term, maybe seasonal, perhaps permanent, changes of location.

Migration

Consider the case of Juan, a young man living in an old house of mud and slate in the forested uplands of Portugal. It has one living room which has no chimney, so the smoke from the fire escapes via the door. The oxen live in the room below. The lofts are full of hay and vegetables. The village has no electricity, no phone, no piped gas or water or sanitation and no road, only a dirt track linking the village to the outside world.

At Christmas and summer, Juan meets his former neighbour who went to find work in a car plant in Paris. He now has a two-storey house in Paris, with garage, a car, colour TV, stereo, and enough spare income to send his daughter to a private school. This neighbour had to sneak across the frontier into France so, like millions of other Portuguese in France, his status is illegal. When he returns to Portugal on holiday he risks being denied permission to return to France.

Draw a diagram like fig. 4.5 and show in the PUSH box the reasons for Juan wanting to leave his home in Portugal. In the

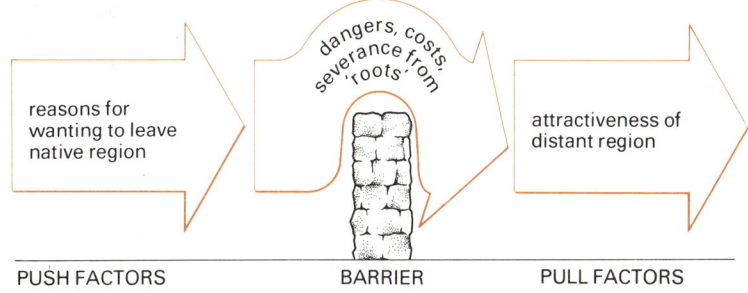

figure 4.5 Migration: pull/push model

PULL box print the reasons for wanting to go to Paris. Show what is represented by the BARRIER. Some migrants meet up with 'intermediate opportunities' which can cause them to settle in a town along their intended journey.

Examine fig. 4.6 to find how many Portuguese now live outside Portugal. If they all returned there would be 30% of the Portuguese work force unemployed. If Juan decided to go to Paris he would be one of the millions of 'guestworkers' in the industrialised regions of Europe. He would also become part of the largest migration in human history: the movement of people from the countryside into cities.

figure 4.6 Portuguese at home and abroad

Rural—urban migration

In 1980 there were just under two billion (2 000 000 000) people living in the world's cities. It is estimated that by the year 2000 there will be 3.2 billion. Of these, over two billion will be in the cities of the third world.

At the start of the 1980s there were something like 75 000 people moving from the country each day to live in the already overcrowded 'third world' cities. It is impossible to provide the necessary *infrastructure* (water supply, roads, sanitation etc.) to keep pace with this rural—urban migration. So the new arrivals move into the 'shanties' like the one in fig. 4.7. The pattern is the same throughout the third world — Calcutta, Karachi, Peking, Shanghai, Seoul, Cairo and Rio de Janeiro will each have between 15 and 30 million people by the end of the century. In 1980 people were arriving in Rio de Janeiro at the rate of 5000 a week.

On arrival, the immigrants usually stay a short while with friends or relations already established in the city. They then move into the shanties on the outskirts. The cities therefore have their poorest inhabitants on the outskirts. How does this compare with the European cities? See fig. 2.7 (page 18).

Juan would intend to be a *temporary* migrant but, of

figure 4.7 A shanty settlement in Bombay

course, many decide to become *permanent* inhabitants of their new homes. Some set off as permanent migrants but become homesick and return. Many families leave Britain every year for a new life in Australia or New Zealand. Like Juan, they leave of their own free will as *voluntary* migrants. This is not always the case: some of the earth's largest and most famous migrations have been *enforced* migrations. From Biblical times through to the expulsion of Asians from Uganda in the 1970s there is a history of enforced migrations. Many of Australia's early white settlers were transported convicts. The state of Israel absorbed many Jews expelled from Europe. So we can see in the pattern of human migration not only differences of distance, frequency and duration, but also of motivation.

Summary

In this chapter we have considered how:

- People move from place to place
- Movement is a response to perceived needs
- There are spatial patterns in human movement
- There are time patterns in human movement
- Some movements are short distance, short stay, temporary, frequent and voluntary
- Some movements are the opposite

The exercises that follow offer examples of different sorts of migrations at various scales, represented by several graphic methods and suggesting some key ideas concerning migration.

Exercises

1 In fig. 4.8 a matrix relates the *length of journey* to the *length of stay*. Copy the matrix and add to it some other movements including:

> A housewife shopping; a Bolivian peasant migrating from the *altiplano* of the High Andes to live in La Paz; a Masai moving with his herds in Kenya; a farmer working in his fields; a Londoner on a day-trip to Brighton; a Vietnamese refugee to the United Kingdom.

Some of these movements are daily, some seasonal, some are 'once for all'. Devise a method of showing on the matrix the *frequency* of each movement.

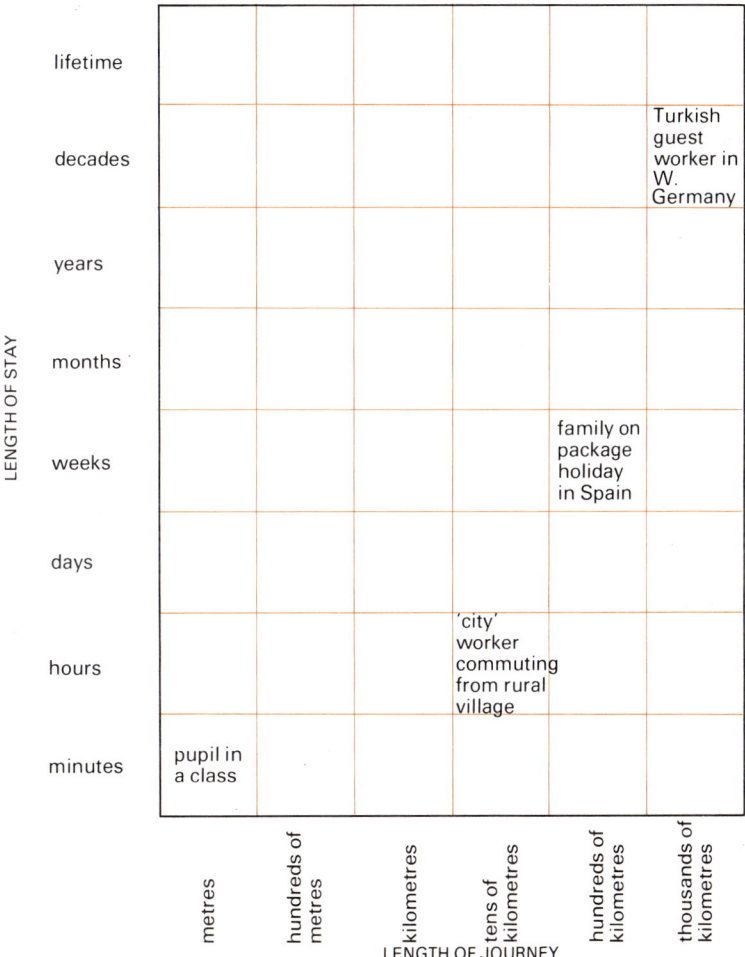

figure 4.8 People and movement

2 The block diagram fig. 4.9A shows in simplified form the Swiss valley of Schachental. On weekdays a hundred people commute from Unterschachen, the main village, to work in Altdorf, the town in the main valley. At weekends, some Altdorf folk travel to Unterschachen and go walking in the hills. Some take the cable car up to an alpine hamlet like Wannelen (fig. 4.9). These journeys are shown by arrows on fig. 4.9A.

In July, about a hundred farmers leave Unterschachen with their cows (and sometimes pigs), working their way up to the summer residences on the alp. In August they reach the upper alp. The milk is churned to butter and cheese. They cut grass for hay. These products they send down the cable way to the valley bottom. Then in September they return to Unterschachen. These seasonal migrations are shown in fig. 4.9B.

Draw a simplified version of fig. 4.9A and show on it the seasonal migration of the cowherds and their animals.

Copy the graph showing the seasonal movement of the cowherds (fig. 4.9B) and give it the title '**Transhumance** in Switzerland.' Add to it, preferably in different colours, some of the following:

the Unterschachen commuters' daily journeys to Altdorf; the Altdorf residents' weekend trips to go walking on the alp; the winter ski parties visiting the valley from outside the region (you may be able to work out the pattern of their movement).

figure 4.9 A. A Swiss Alpine valley B. Graph showing the movement of farmers with animals in a Swiss valley

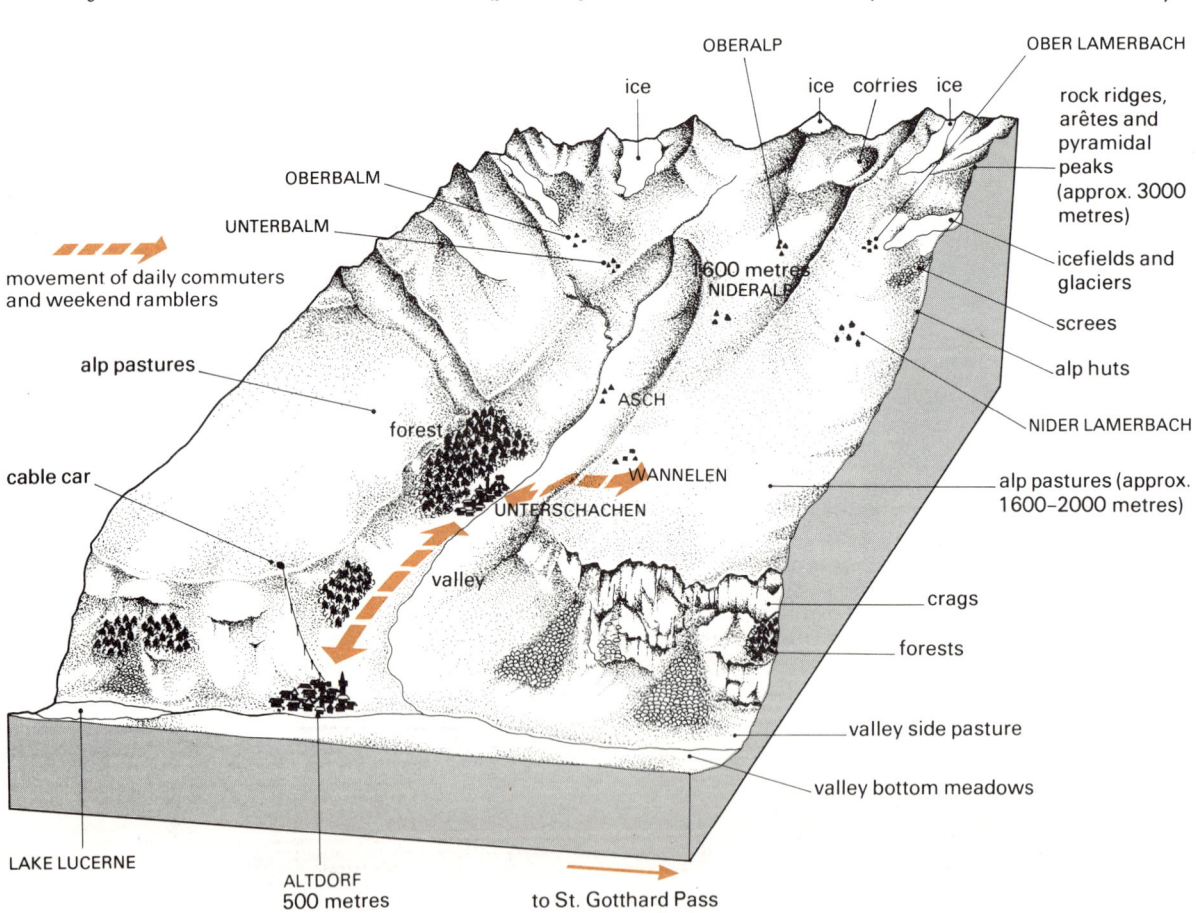

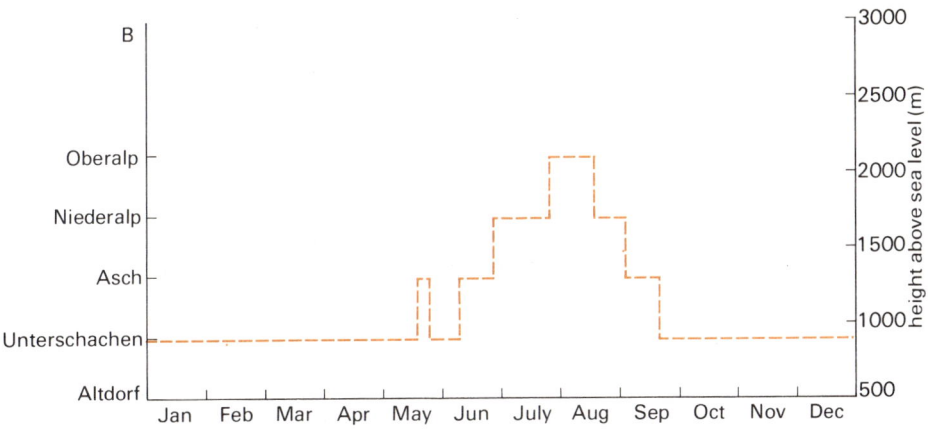

Draw a simple outline sketch of the photograph, which shows a Swiss Alpine valley. Identify and label (i) a valley bottom village, (ii) an alp pasture, (iii) winter ski slopes, (iv) a ski resort, (v) a road down the valley to the main valley town, (vi) ice fields and glaciers. Use arrows to show the likely movements of farmers, holidaymakers and commuters in this part of this valley.

3 Plot on an outline map of the world some of the major world migrations such as:

British to Australia and New Zealand; Spaniards and Portuguese to Latin America; Irish to USA; Dutch and British to South Africa; African slaves to the West Indies and Southern USA.

4 The map in fig. 4.10 shows migrations *to* the United Kingdom in 1976. Use the table to draw a map showing *net* movement between the UK and the regions listed. Describe the pattern revealed by the map.

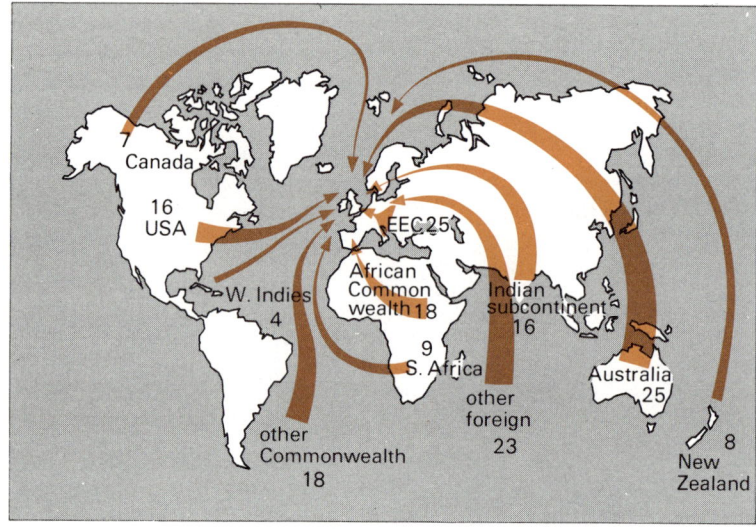

UK migration 1976 (in thousands)

		IN	OUT	NET
Old Commonwealth	Australia	25	32	−7
	Canada	7	23	−16
	New Zealand	8	9	−1
New Commonwealth	Africa	18	11	+7
	Indian subcontinent	16	6	+10
	West Indies	4	4	0
	Other	18	10	+8
Foreign	EEC	25	31	−6
	Other European	11	13	−2
	USA	16	21	−5
	S. Africa	9	21	−12
	Other	23	31	−8
		180	212	−32

figure 4.10 Migration to and from the UK, 1976

5 A variety of types of migration is shown in fig. 4.11. Write a paragraph about each *or* draw an annotated version of each.

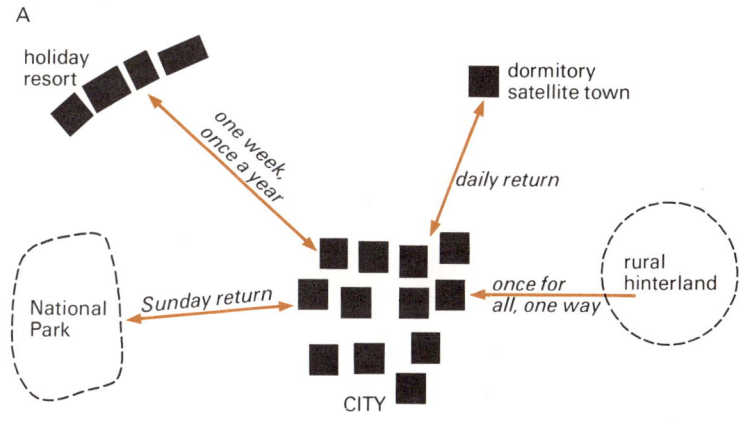

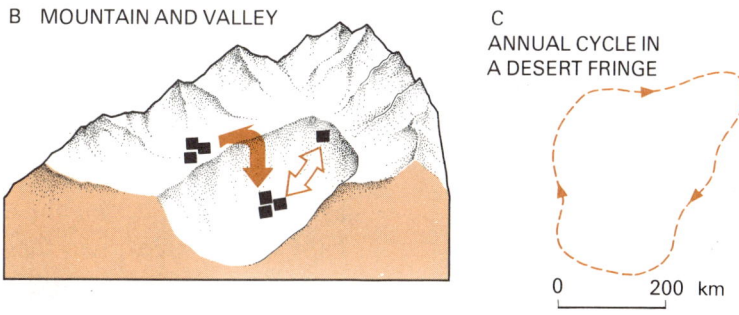

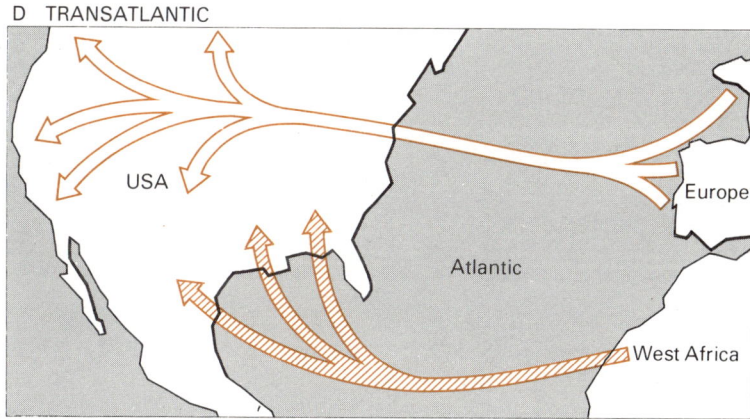

figure 4.11 Types of migration

6 Ask your teachers and/or classmates and/or neighbours
(a) where they live now and
(b) where they have lived before.
Plot this on a map. You may have to draw arrows coming into your home region from other parts of the country.

Describe the pattern shown by your map of the migrations of your teachers/classmates/neighbours.

5 Worlds apart

In fig. 5.1 the Japanese lady and her camera have travelled thousands of miles on a journey costing more than the Masai lady will earn in a lifetime. The two women do not exchange a word. The Masai lady does not even look up — she may be puzzled as to why she is being photographed. She will certainly be unable to visualise the Japanese lady's life style.

This photograph illustrates a lot of the ideas we have been discussing in previous chapters. Some of them are summarised in fig. 5.2. The photo also raises a lot of questions. What do the two women have in common? And in what essential features do they differ? Both are female and middle-aged but beyond that they could hardly be more different. How are we to explain these differences?

figure 5.1 A Japanese lady photographs a Masai lady in Kenya

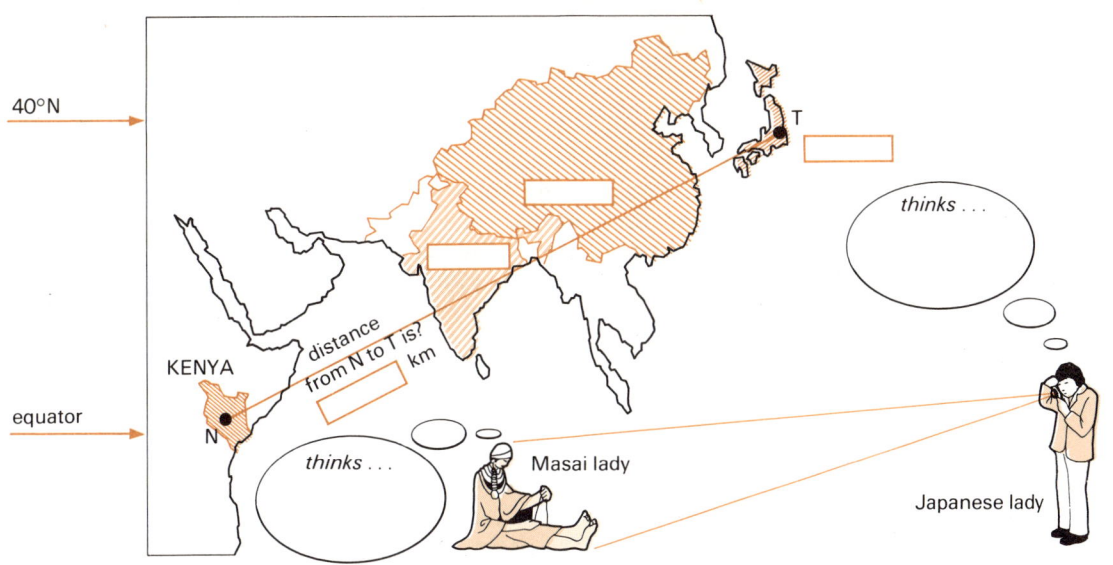

A MASAI LADY	WHO ARE THEY?	A JAPANESE LADY
(describe her physical appearance)	WHAT ARE THEY LIKE?	(describe her physical appearance)
Caucasoid – Negroid	WHICH RACES?	Mongoloid
Kenya's population is _____* (there are 150 000 Masai)	HOW MANY PEOPLE LIVE IN THEIR COUNTRIES?	Japan's population is _____*
Masailand has a population density of 2.5 people per sq.km. This is a _____ density	HOW CROWDED ARE THEIR COUNTRIES?	Japan has a population density of 270 people per sq.km. This is a _____ density
(Remember, the Masai are cattle rearers who often move from place to place in search of pasture. They just manage to feed themselves.)	HOW DO THEY LIVE? (use words like subsistence, urbanised, sedentary, nomadic, pastoralists)	(The Japanese have a highly advanced, industrialised 'western' economy. 80% of them live in towns.)
KENYA population structure pyramid	WHAT ARE THEIR POPULATION STRUCTURES LIKE? Compare the two pyramids for Kenya and Japan. What do you conclude about their birth and death rates?	JAPAN population structure pyramid
Kenya's GNP per capita is $_____*. Does this lady reflect this? Is she above or below this average?	WHAT ARE THEIR LEVELS OF PROSPERITY? +	Japan's GNP per capita is $_____*. Does this woman reflect this? Is she above or below this average?

see pages 106-7   + fill this in after reading chapter 6

figure 5.2 Kenyan/Japanese contrasts

Exercises

1 Copy fig. 5.2, leaving enough space to answer the questions. Fill in the spaces.

2 Try to discover your friends' or your family's perceptions of the Japanese, the Kenyans or the Masai. One way is to do a 'word-association' exercise. Give each person a blank sheet of paper and ask them to write quickly all the words and thoughts which come to mind when you give them a certain word. You then say 'Masai' or 'Japanese'. You can process the results, perhaps draw a histogram, to show 'Our mental image of the Japanese' etc. Does everyone have the same image?

3 Figure 5.3 shows a Masai family. They have just emerged from their manyatta (the Masai house) to be photographed. Can you guess the occupations of the two sons standing on each side of the father?* If this photo alters the impression given by fig. 5.1, make a note on your copy of fig. 5.2.

Figure 5.3 This is a Masai chief with his sons and daughters

4 The Japanese, the Masai and Kenya often feature in newspaper and magazine articles, TV programmes and holiday brochures. Collect newscuttings, photos etc., and add them to your notes on fig. 5.2.

As an example, the *Sunday Times* of 14th November 1982 showed a photograph of thousands of tiny statues in a Japanese temple, explaining that each represented one of the 600 000 babies aborted in Japan each year. Look at the population pyramid. Make some comment in your notes on fig. 5.2.

5 Draw a simple annotated sketch version of fig. 5.1, analysing the photo. Print underneath it a title which conveys the content and the ideas aroused by the photo.

Add a P.S. at the bottom, listing any ways in which your own ideas have changed as a result of this chapter.

6 Write a short story or report which includes a chain of events leading in the end to a Masai woman, like the one in the photograph, photographing a Japanese woman in Tokyo.

* One son (on the chief's left, wearing jeans) is an agricultural adviser; the other (in a suit) is a lawyer.

Summary

In this chapter we have considered the following ideas. Think of examples of each of them and make a note of them for revision.

- We must beware of stereotypes
- Photographs can be used to convey ideas or to reinforce prejudices or to challenge outdated attitudes
- Some people travel large distances just to look at other people
- Some people wish to retain traditional lifestyles
- Some people wish to change traditional lifestyles
- Some people live in balance with their environment
- Some people put great strain on finite resources
- Modern transport methods can bring together people who have contrasting lifestyles

Urban Tokyo

6 Patterns of wealth and poverty

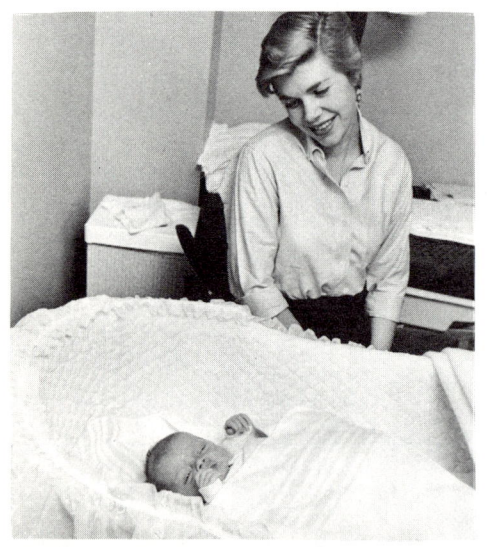

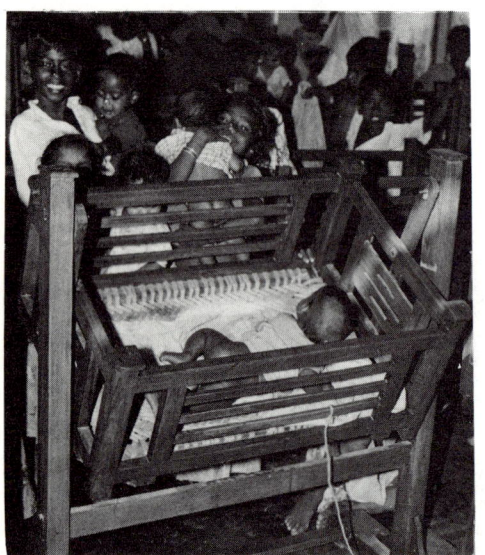

figure 6.1 A. A baby born in the USA
B. A baby born in India

What evidence is there in these two photographs to support the statement at the start of this chapter?

A baby born in a village in India can expect a very different life from a baby born at the same moment in a Dallas, USA, maternity hospital. (See fig. 6.1.) For a start, it has less chance of surviving birth. If it does, it cannot expect as long a life. In material terms, it cannot expect as much out of life. This is a dramatic way of illustrating extreme contrasts in 'quality of life' or 'well-being'.

The quality of life

We are all familiar with the lifestyles of wealthy Americans as portrayed on film and TV serials. We are also familiar with the image (but perhaps not in such detail) of starving children in poorer countries. If we are to clarify our ideas and understand how these contrasts arose we need to know what to measure and how to map it.

Make a list of the things *you* would use to measure the quality of *your* life. This will reveal a lot about your own standards and values. You might then compare your list with those of your classmates. Your list might include colour TV, annual holidays abroad, a second family car. It would probably not mention such things as an hour's daily journey to fetch water or how to obtain food in a dry season. If we are to measure the quality of life of different groups of people we shall have to decide on measurements which are easy to obtain and readily understood. An example might be **life expectancy**.

Measuring well-being

Figure 6.2 shows variations in one particular aspect of 'well-being' in an English city. In the All Saints district, 62 per cent of the houses lacked indoor water closets, whereas in West Shirley, only a few kilometres away, everyone had an indoor W.C. After the exercises in chapter 4, you will realise that whatever index is mapped (social class, two-car families etc.), you can expect to find similar patterns: it seems that the

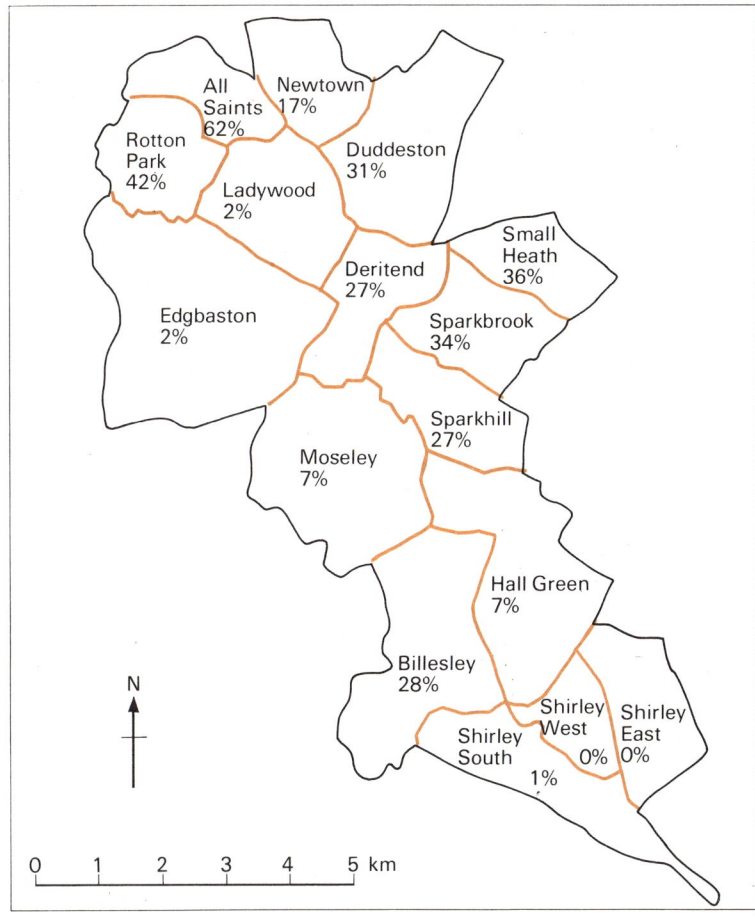

figure 6.2 Variations in the percentage of houses with no inside W.C. in a transect of wards from central to south Birmingham (data from the 1971 census)

figure 6.3 Variations in the index of well-being (a measure of a number of criteria that indicate material quality of life) for the major planning regions of Great Britain

quality of a person's life is closely related to the neighbourhood in which he lives.

Figure 6.3 shows the variations in 'well-being' for the various planning regions of Great Britain. Which region scores highest? Rank the regions from highest to lowest and see what sort of pattern emerges. Note that All Saints, Birmingham, is in the West Midlands — a region which scores well *above* the national average. The map also suggests a south–north gradient which can be plotted on a graph (fig. 6.4).

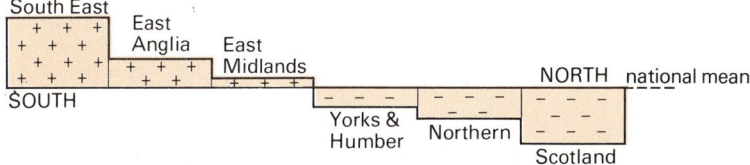

figure 6.4 Index of well-being: deviation from the national mean on a south to north transect

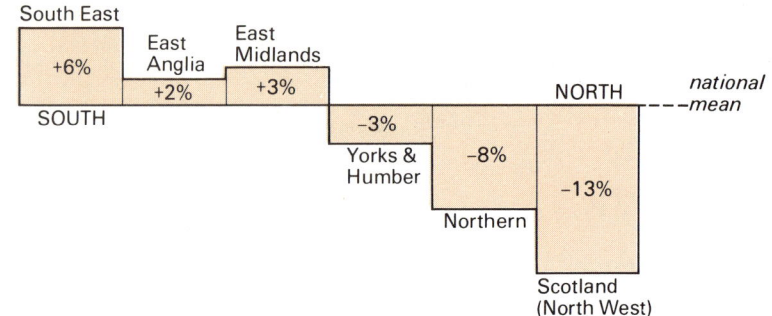

figure 6.5 Net income: deviation from the national mean on a south to north transect

Compare the graph with fig. 6.5 which shows deviations from the **national mean income**. This is the total national income divided by the number of workers. It is also called **per capita income** (income per head).

table 6.1 *Per capita income for a selection of countries (US $)*

Over 1500	USA, France, Great Britain, Italy, Libya, Japan, Australia
1001–1500	USSR, Ireland, Poland
801–1000	Venezuela, Argentina, Spain, Rumania, Greece
601–800	Chile, Cuba
451–600	South Africa, Yugoslavia, Mexico
301–450	Turkey, Mongolia, Zambia, Brazil, Peru, Saudi Arabia
151–300	Morocco, Algeria, Angola, Uruguay, Thailand
0–150	India, China, Uganda, Mali, Afghanistan

The most commonly used measure of *national* wealth is the **gross national product** (GNP): the total amount of goods and services produced each year by that country. The GNP for all the South American countries in 1980 is shown in fig. 6.6. Which has the highest GNP? Is this the wealthiest country? Or could a country with a lower GNP but with fewer people to share it be more prosperous? Draw up a table ranking the countries according to GNP. Now use the data in table 6.2 and rank the countries according to **GNP per capita** (the GNP divided by the population of the country).

When dealing with GNP, remember:

1. the figures are averages within which there can be a tremendous range;

2. the GNP per capita can be distorted by an influx of money in the form of armaments given by major powers, such as

the USA and USSR, or investment by a multinational corporation, which scarcely affects the real economy;

3. GNP per capita may not be a reliable guide to the quality of life, as the figures in table 6.4 show. (PQLI means Physical Quality of Life Index).

The Physical Quality of Life Index was produced by the Overseas Development Council in Washington. It is based on **infant mortality**, **life expectancy** and **basic literacy**. These are all matters of fundamental concern, whatever the commercial success of the country.

figure 6.6 Gross National Product figures in US $1000 millions (billions) for the countries of South America (1980)

table 6.2 GNP per capita for South American countries, 1980 (from **The 1981 World Bank Atlas**)

	GNP per capita (US$)
Argentina	2390
Bolivia	570
Brazil	2050
Chile	2160
Colombia	1180
Ecuador	1220
French Guiana	2880
Guyana	690
Paraguay	1340
Peru	930
Suriname	2840
Uruguay	2820
Venezuela	3630

table 6.3 GNP per capita for a selection of countries

	US$
Federal Republic of Germany	7510
United Kingdom	4180
Greece	2570
Turkey	1010
Peru	840
USA	7880
Bangladesh	90
Singapore	2580
Egypt	280
Saudi Arabia	4420

table 6.4

	GNP per capita	PQLI
India	133	43
Nigeria	297	25
Sri Lanka	179	82

Which of the three countries has the highest GNP per capita? Which has the highest PQLI?

49

The World Bank uses GNP per capita to divide the world into rich, middle and poor countries (see fig. 6.8). We often hear people using the terms 'first', 'second' and 'third world'. These mean:

1. **The 'first world'** The 'free' or 'western' or 'capitalist' world of the 'Atlantic Bloc' plus Japan, Australasia and South Africa.
2. **The 'second world'** The 'Communist Bloc' of Eastern Europe, USSR, China, Cuba and Vietnam.
3. **The 'third world'** All the remaining countries, many of which are politically non-aligned. Some of these are often referred to as 'backward', 'underdeveloped' or 'developing'. Some third world countries have more wealth than some countries in groups 1 and 2.

This list reads very much like 'us', and 'them' and 'the rest'.

figure 6.7 A. Nomad's tent

B. Oil Sheikh's jet

Both the nomad and the Sheikh live in Saudi Arabia, which has a GNP per capita of $9960

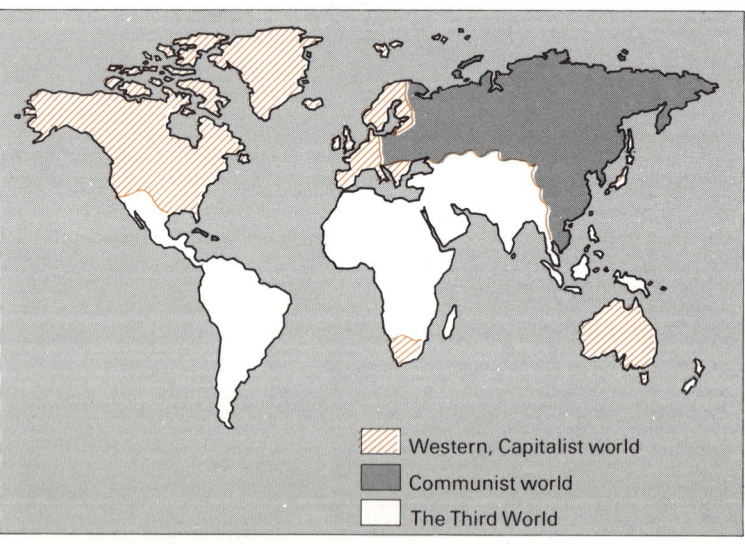

Western, Capitalist world

Communist world

The Third World

figure 6.8 First, second and third worlds

A lot of people find titles such as 'first' and 'backward' unacceptable.

Groups 1 and 2 are often referred to collectively as 'The North' while group 3 is called 'The South'. These labels come from *'North-South': a programme for survival*, the report of the Independent Commission on Development Issues. The commission was chaired by Willy Brandt (a former West German President) and included Edward Heath (a former British Prime Minister).

The Brandt report, as it is known, called for an international development tax to be levied on nations, just as income tax is levied on individuals. The tax would raise $30 billion to add to the $40 billion already given to Less Developed Countries, in order to:

1. explore for energy and minerals;
2. increase food production;
3. develop transport;
4. improve technical and medical facilities.

The aim would be to:

> fight poverty, disease and misery;
> increase world trade;
> decrease the danger of world war.

The initial response of world governments was discouraging because the recession in the early 1980s prompted them to reduce their contributions to world aid programmes. The flow of aid from 'north' to 'south' was at that time only a tiny part of the income of the wealthy nations. The United Nations had agreed in 1970 that rich countries should provide 0.7% of their GNP in aid to LDCs. The UK percentage was 0.51% in 1979 and fell to 0.34% in 1980. This was less than half the sum agreed in 1970.

TYPES OF AID

bilateral government to government

multilateral via international agencies like the World Bank

private investment by companies, usually with profit in mind

voluntary given by organisations like OXFAM with no strings attached

tied aid money to be spent on goods and services from the donating country

grants awards to help with specific projects

loans money to be paid back at low interest rates

Summary

If you look back over this chapter you will find that it covered the following ideas:

- There are great contrasts in well-being at all scales
- We can measure, map and graph well-being
- Patterns of wealth distribution are repeated at all scales
- In some places, prosperity gradients (the differences between the 'richest' and 'poorest' in the area) are very steep
- Steep prosperity gradients produce
  - population movements
  - social disadvantage
  - political unrest
- The flow of wealth does not necessarily even out prosperity gradients

Exercises

1 Infant mortality in the USA is mapped in fig. 6.9. Which state has the lowest rate? What is the California rate? Are there any surprises? What is meant by 'others'? Write some reasons for the different infant mortality rates for 'whites' and 'others'.

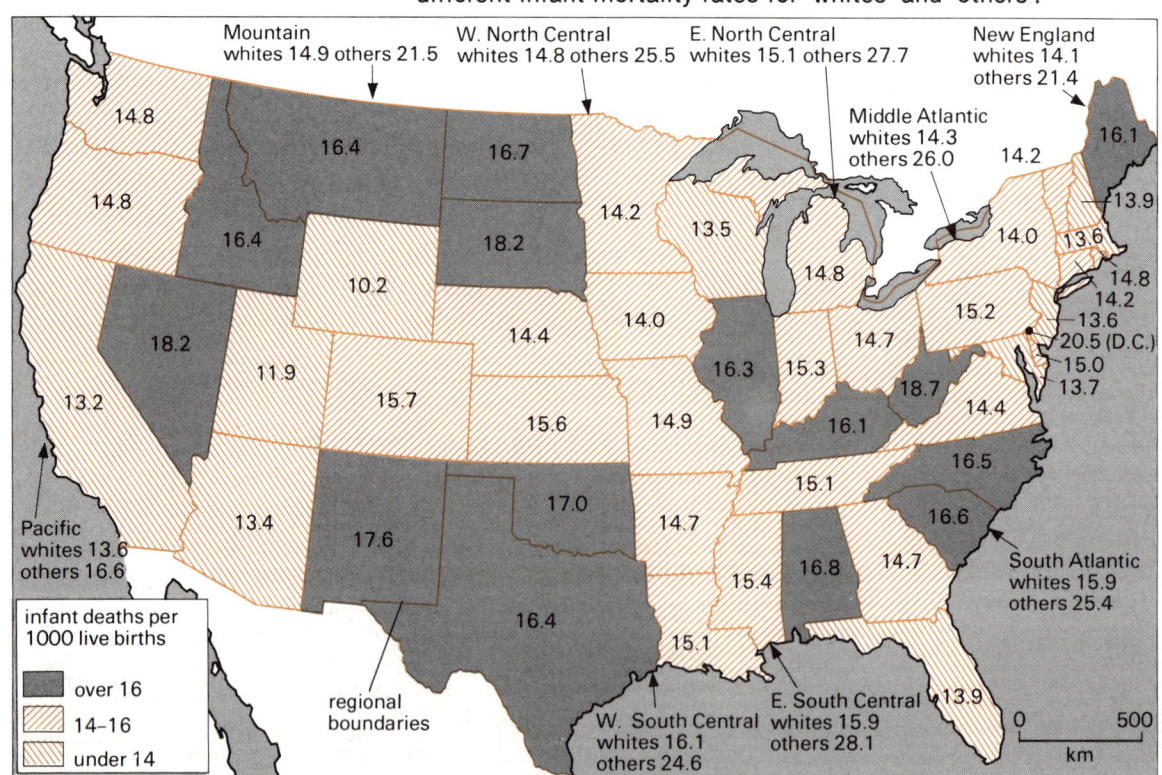

figure 6.9 Infant mortality in the USA

2 Describe the variations in the physical quality of life in Nairobi as shown in fig. 6.10. Say how Nairobi compares with our model in fig. 2.7, page 18. Look up the GNP per capita for Kenya and comment on the physical quality of life of residents in Parklands and Pumwani.

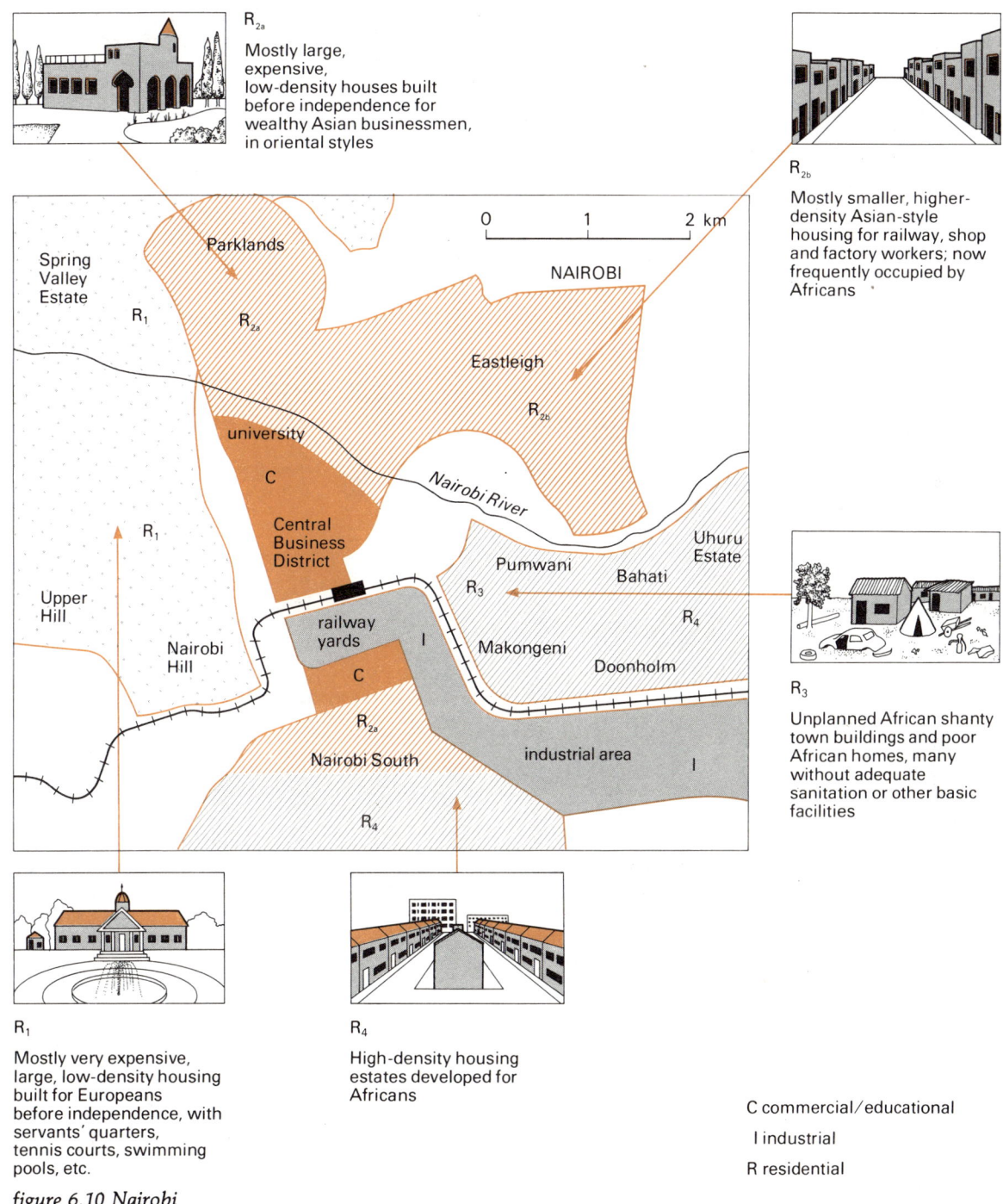

R_{2a}
Mostly large, expensive, low-density houses built before independence for wealthy Asian businessmen, in oriental styles

R_{2b}
Mostly smaller, higher-density Asian-style housing for railway, shop and factory workers; now frequently occupied by Africans

R₃
Unplanned African shanty town buildings and poor African homes, many without adequate sanitation or other basic facilities

R₁
Mostly very expensive, large, low-density housing built for Europeans before independence, with servants' quarters, tennis courts, swimming pools, etc.

R₄
High-density housing estates developed for Africans

C commercial/educational

I industrial

R residential

figure 6.10 Nairobi

3 (a) Write a comparison between figs. 6.4 and 6.5.

(b) Figure 11.3 (page 106) shows GNP per capita. Select some countries from *one* continent and find each country's average latitude from an atlas. (You should try to include the most northerly countries and the most southerly in that continent.)

Plot on a graph the GNP per capita and the latitude of each country. (See fig. 6.11.) What does your graph reveal? Is there a gradient north–south as the Brandt Report suggests? Examine fig. 6.8 and compare the distribution of poorer countries with (i) latitude, (ii) location of former colonies of European countries.

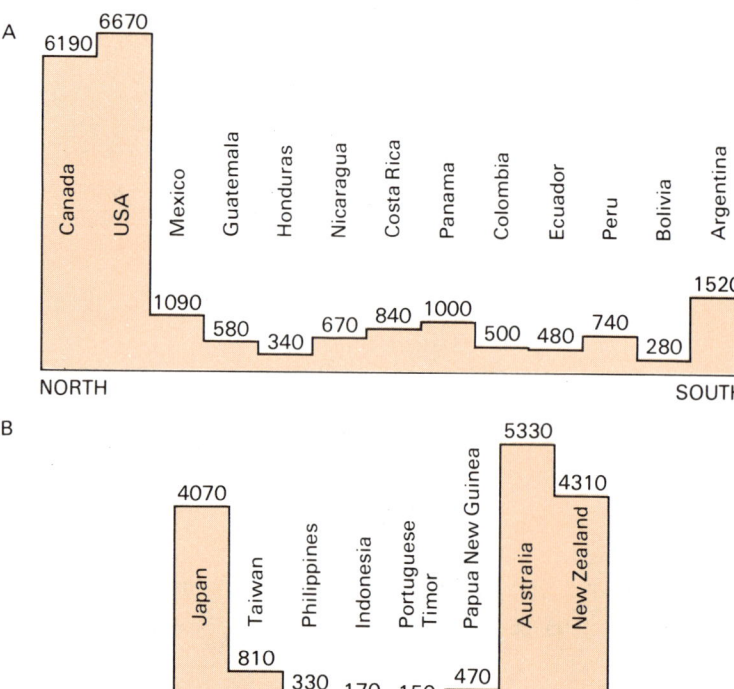

figure 6.11 *Two north–south transects to illustrate variations of GNP per capita*

4 Devise a method of drawing a prosperity profile (see fig. 2.6) across your own city or region using either (a) house prices in newspapers, (b) perceived indicators such as double garages, or (c) statistical records such as the census records.

You could test an idea such as 'the quality of life decreases from highland to lowland'.

5 Describe the effect on a country's GNP after:

(a) a major oilfield is discovered.

(b) a war destroys roads, railways and factories.

(c) supplies of consumer goods are limited by government policy.

(d) a natural disaster (e.g. earthquake, floods, hurricane).

7 Development in action

Mr Maputo's farm is in a part of Southern Africa which at the turn of the century was known as 'the granary of Matabeleland'. His grandparents practised **shifting subsistence agriculture**: when the crop yields fell they shifted to newly cleared lands leaving the **fallow** land to recover for several years. (See fig. 7.2.) Occasionally a surplus of grain (millet or sorghum) would be traded with neighbouring tribes or European settlers. But there was normally no need for cash in their traditional way of life (see fig. 7.3).

figure 7.1 *The never-ending task of drawing up well water on a farm in southern Africa*

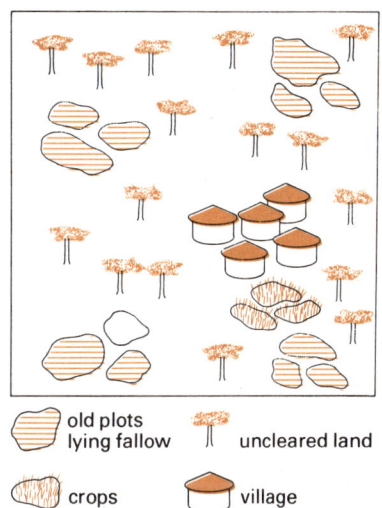

old plots lying fallow   uncleared land

crops   village

figure 7.2 *Shifting agriculture*

Shifting agriculture needs a lot of land so that fields can lie fallow long enough to recover their fertility. How would farmers in the village in fig. 7.2 be affected if they lost some of their land to white settlers?

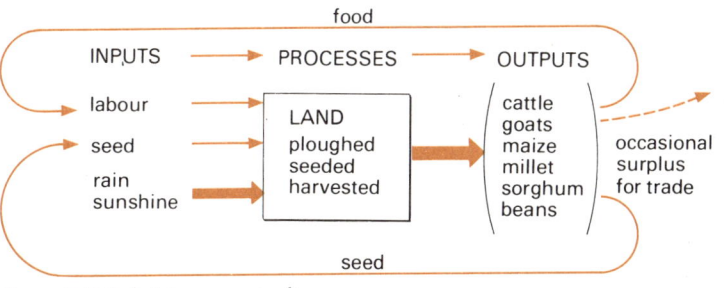

figure 7.3 *Subsistence agriculture*

Redraw fig. 7.3, incorporating the developments resulting from stages 1, 2 and 3 of the colonial phase

DEVELOPMENTS DURING THE COLONIAL PHASE

(approximately 1900–1966)
1. Some of the land was allocated to white settlers.
2. The Protectorate Government imposed a Hut Tax. This meant:
   (a) the farmers needed a regular income to pay the tax
   (b) some of the products were thereby lost from the system.
3. The mines in South Africa needed a lot of labourers.

Now the only way to ensure a regular cash income was for the young men to go to the South African mines. Look at fig. 3.15 and then add to your copy of fig. 7.3 a simplified population pyramid with a note on 'the absentee males' and the effect of male migration on the traditional way of life. The chief of the tribe summarised these effects in 1936:

Lack of manpower to work the land

Lowering of food supply for the tribe

Tuberculosis: of the 400 boys going to the mines in January and February, 20 had to return with chest trouble.

Immorality as a result of husbands and wives being separated.

Young men lose contact with tribe and lose respect for elders.

Political independence

When the country (Bechuanaland) became politically independent in 1966 (as Botswana) it remained economically dependent on the migration of males to South African mines. Half the country's foreign currency earnings came from absentee miners.

This type of development was common in areas colonised by Europeans. It made these regions economically dependent on European countries. What effect would it have on
(a) the population structure of the region?
(b) family life?
(c) social stability?
(d) efficiency of farming?

Mr Maputo's farm is two hours walk from the nearest water supply. Each day the women and girls:

fetch water,

walk to the field to work,

return to 'stamp' the corn and cook a meal.

The boys and men:

> drive the animals to the water hole and back to the
>   safety of the kraal,
> collect wood (the only fuel) for the fire.

All the family's time and energy is spent tending animals and growing crops. When the rains fail they go hungry. If ever there is a small surplus, they have no access to market because the only transport is bullock cart, the only road a dirt track which washes out in the rains. Mr Maputo and his neighbours are a long way from a doctor. They are particularly vulnerable to pneumonia and tuberculosis, and to accidents.

The development decades

During the 1960s and 1970s a great many changes occurred in Mr Maputo's district.

Emergency aid was made available by Oxfam, Red Cross etc., during the droughts of the 1960s.

Development aid financed projects such as
>   a bore hole providing water for the village
>   a clinic
>   a school
>   an 'all-purpose machine' to carry wood and water
>   a water catchment tank (see fig. 7.4)

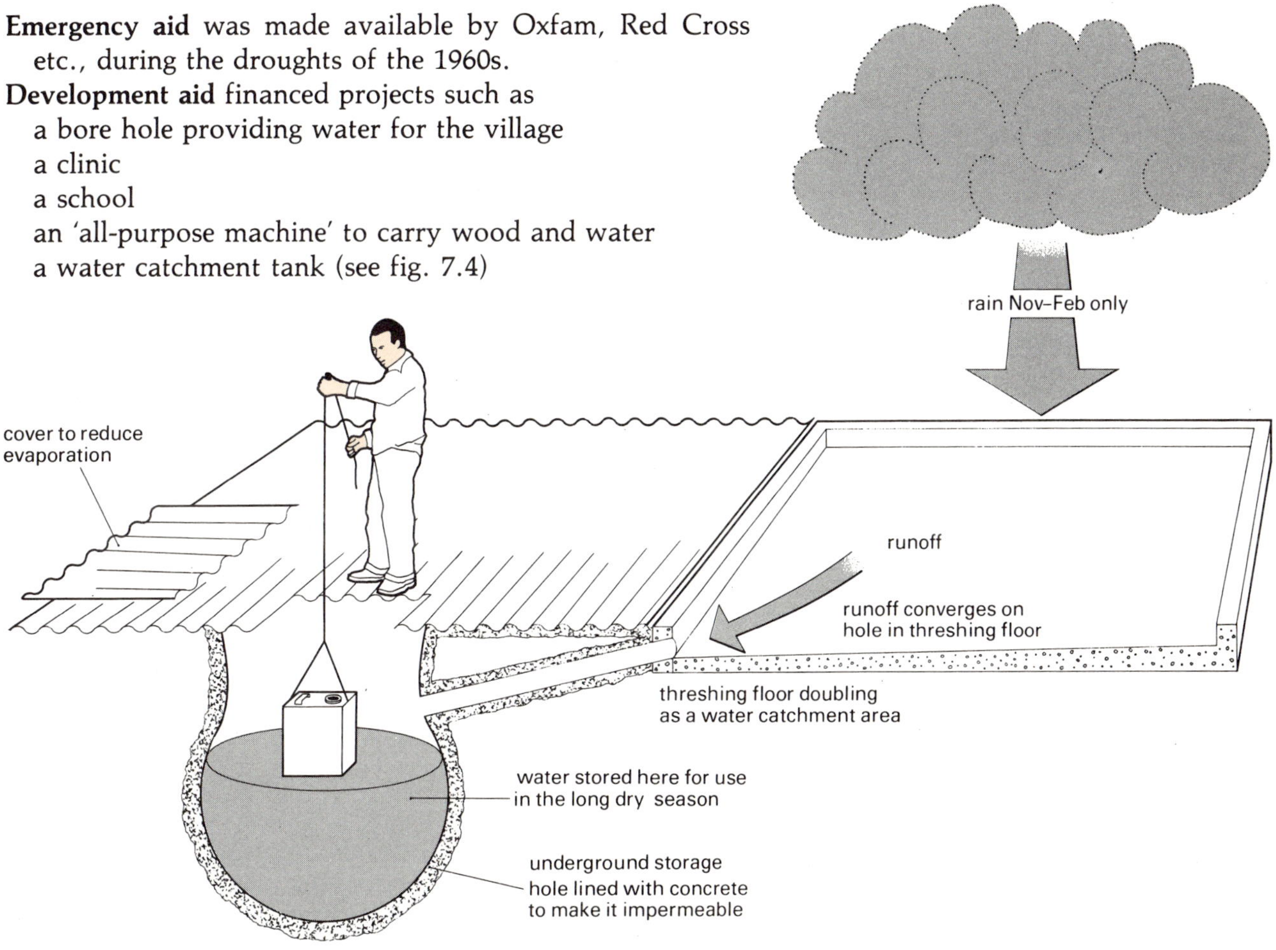

rain Nov–Feb only

cover to reduce evaporation

runoff

runoff converges on hole in threshing floor

threshing floor doubling as a water catchment area

water stored here for use in the long dry season

underground storage hole lined with concrete to make it impermeable

figure 7.4 A water catchment tank. Like the 'all-purpose machine', this is an example of 'relevant technology'

How do you think these developments will affect the life of Mr
Maputo's family?

agricultural advisers who introduced
- dipping and inoculation of animals
- pest and disease control for crops
- controlled grazing
- fertilising the soil

a new copper mine, which was sunk nearby, necessitating

a road to the railhead — this gave access to the abbatoir and meat plant at Lobatse (over 100 km away).

A lot of countries have undergone developments similar to Mr Maputo's country, Botswana. They are often referred to as **less developed countries** (LDCs).

Consider the information in fig. 7.5 and then copy and complete this table:

CHARACTERISTICS OF LESS-DEVELOPED COUNTRIES
GNP per capita . . . .
% of population in agriculture . . . .
% of population in manufacturing . . . .
% of population in services . . . .
Types of farming . . . .
Types of manufacturing . . . .
Birth rate . . . .
Death rate . . . .
Life expectancy . . . .
Population structure . . . .
% living in towns . . . .
Health . . . .
Literacy . . . .
Infrastructure levels . . . .
Role of religion . . . .
Role of women . . . .
Level of technology . . . .

Nepal, amongst the 30 least developed countries of the world, has a GNP/capita of $130, a low literacy rate (20%), a high crude birth rate (47°/∞), large number of dependent children (43% of the population is under 14), a large percentage of rural inhabitants (93%) and chronic poverty (36% earn less than 15 pence a day). There were only 562 doctors for 15 million people in 1981.

You may need to add to or alter this table later in the chapter.

INDICATOR	ROSTOW STAGE 1	ROSTOW STAGE 3	ROSTOW STAGE 5
SECTORS OF THE ECONOMY **1** Primary sector – farming, forestry, mining, quarrying etc. **2** Secondary sector – manufacturing and processing **3** Tertiary sector – administration, transport, commerce, welfare etc.	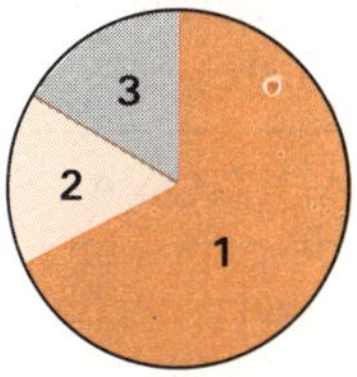	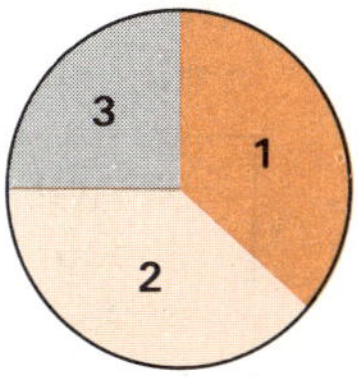	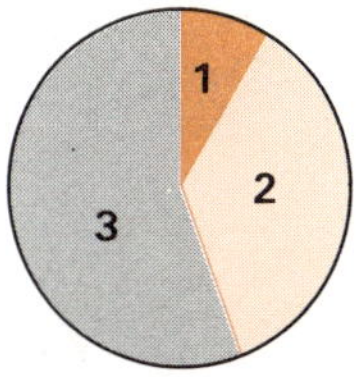
PERCENTAGE OF POPULATION LIVING IN TOWNS **U** urban population living in towns and cities **R** rural population, living in the countryside	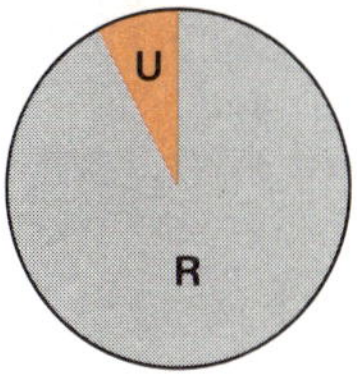	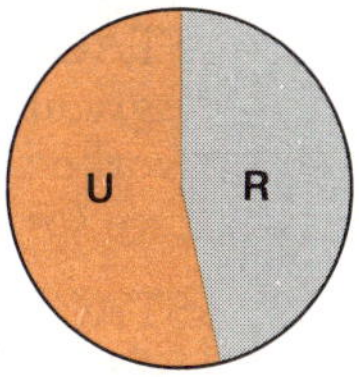	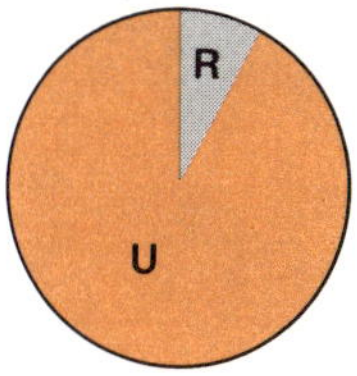
POPULATION PYRAMIDS *see chapter 3, pages 27 – 8* **M** males **F** females	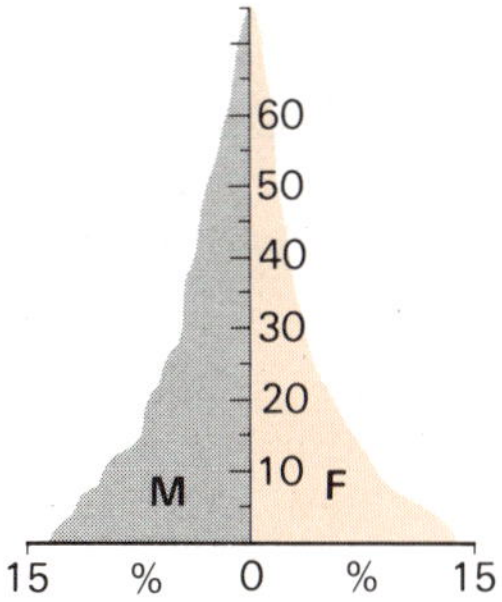	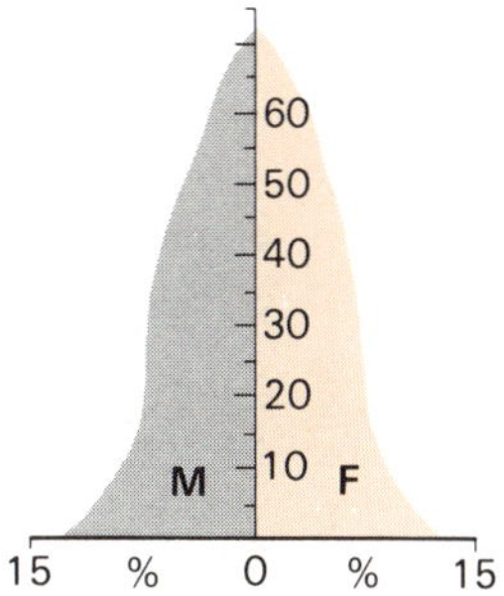	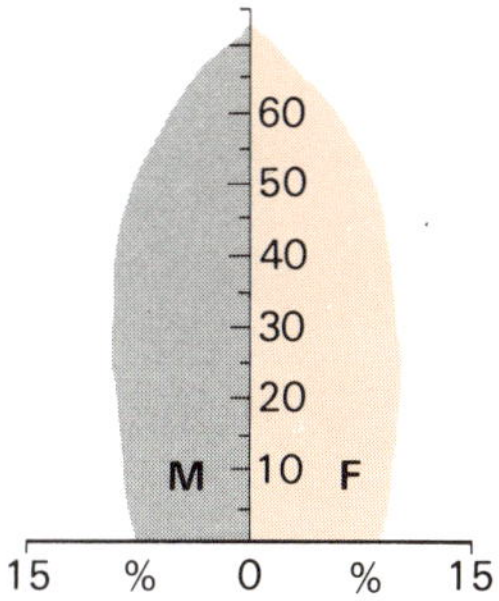
ROAD AND RAIL NETWORK DEVELOPMENT —— rail —— road ● major towns and cities	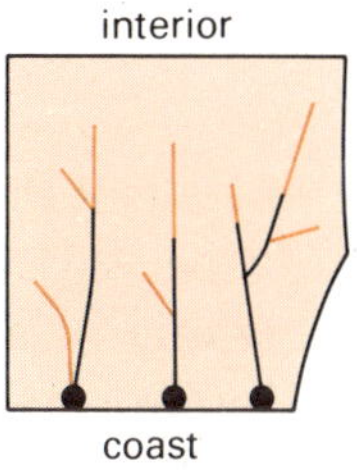 interior coast	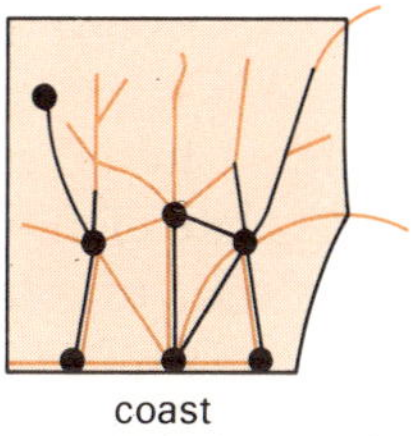 coast	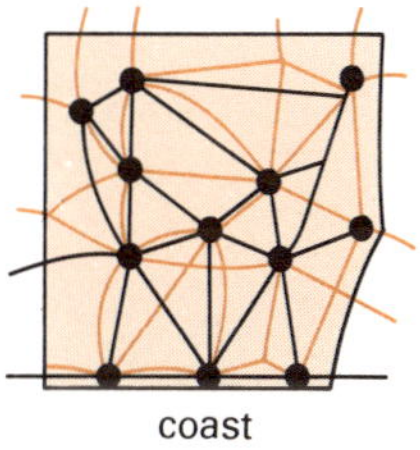 coast
TECHNOLOGY Whilst it is hard to generalise, increasing economic development is associated with increasing levels of technology	 **low technology** e.g. waterwheels, shadufs, ox ploughs, basin irrigation, horse transport, windmills, charcoal furnaces, pottery, hand-woven fabrics	 **medium technology** e.g. tractors, fertilisers, electricity generation, steel, shipbuilding, ore smelting, bridge and railway construction, simple electronics, food processing, irrigation projects, simple mass production	 **high technology** e.g. advanced electronics, aerospace, computers, motor vehicles, special alloys, pharmaceuticals, medical equipment, scientific research and development

figure 7.5 Indicators of development level

How countries may develop

The ways in which countries may develop were expressed in a model by W. W. Rostow:

> **STAGE 1 THE TRADITIONAL SOCIETY**
> A poor country, as described on page 55. Limited agricultural improvement. Low level of technology, health and education. Poor infrastructure. Simple forms of social organisation based on local cultures and religions. Wealth concentrated in the hands of a few.
>
> **STAGE 2 THE PRECONDITIONS FOR TAKE-OFF**
> Agriculture is improved. The additional food supports workers in the secondary and tertiary sectors. The infrastructure (of transport, water and power supplies) develops.
>
> **STAGE 3 TAKE-OFF INTO SELF-SUSTAINED ECONOMIC GROWTH.**
> One or more manufacturing industries grows rapidly. A shift from primary (e.g. mining, fishing, agriculture) to secondary activities.
>
> **STAGE 4 THE DRIVE TO MATURITY**
> The wealth from new activities feeds into all parts of the economy. Industry diversifies. Services like hospitals and schools develop.
>
> **STAGE 5 THE AGE OF HIGH MASS CONSUMPTION**
> A shift from production of basic industrial commodities (steel, chemicals, textiles, machinery) to durable consumer goods (cars, washing machines, TV sets) and high technology products (computers, aerospace), luxury goods (cosmetics, fashions) and services (entertainment, welfare, tourism, recreation).

In this model of development the UK reached stage 2 in the late eighteenth century (the Agricultural Revolution). 'Take-off' (the Industrial Revolution) saw a shift from farming to manufacturing. 'Maturity' was reached in the mid-nineteenth century and the age of 'high mass consumption' in the 1930's.

This model is drawn from the histories of countries in the 'first and second' worlds. It is *wrongly* often taken to imply that:

> The process of development has a beginning and an end.
> Countries *ought to* develop in this way.
> Countries can 'go it alone' with no international contacts.
> The third world ought to (a) help the first and second world countries to stay highly developed, (b) try to catch up with them.

But with all its failings the model provides ideas which help our understanding of development (see table 7.1).

table 7.1 Rostow's Model applied to a selection of countries

Country	Approximate date of reaching stage in Rostow model		
	Stage 3	Stage 4	Stage 5
Britain	1800	1850	1930
France	1860	1910	1950
USA	1860	1910	1920
Germany	1870	1910	1950
Sweden	1890	1930	1945
Japan	1900	1940	1955
USSR	1920	1950	1980?
Canada	1920	1925	1930
Australia	1930	1930	1930
India	1960	—	—
Bangladesh	—	—	—

Progress through the various stages of development can be represented in a variety of ways as shown in fig. 7.5.

As a country begins to develop there is often a concentration of investment in a 'prestige project' such as an aluminium smelter, a steel works or a meat cannery. This new centre of development acts as a **growth pole**. From the growth pole, the newly created wealth should spread through the surrounding countryside and its population. Figure 7.6A shows this process.

A

THE 'SWASH' EFFECT
This is the intended outcome of the siting of a 'growth pole' in an underdeveloped country or region. Roads and railways spread wealth inland, developing the hinterland.

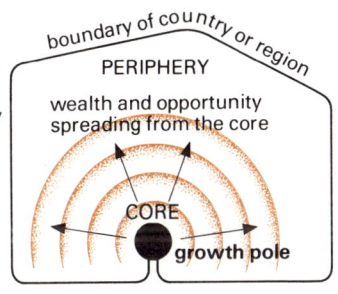

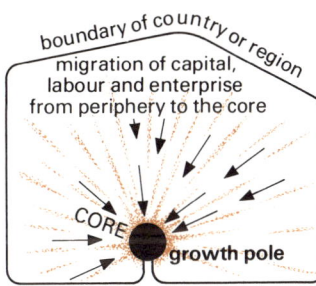

THE 'BACKWASH' EFFECT
This is the possible unplanned and unintended outcome of the siting of a 'growth pole' in an underdeveloped country or region. This creates two levels of wealth, and so is called dualism. Instead of spreading wealth inland as planned, the growth pole actually drains wealth from the surrounding hinterland.

B

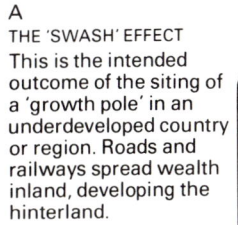

INTENDED OUTCOME

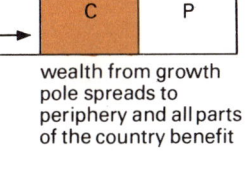

before the development of the 'growth pole'

wealth from growth pole spreads to periphery and all parts of the country benefit

UNINTENDED OUTCOME

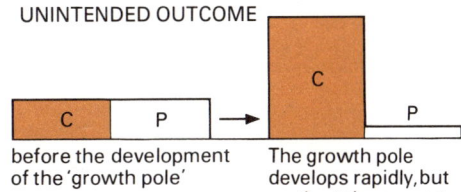

before the development of the 'growth pole'

The growth pole develops rapidly, but partly at the expense of the periphery which actually becomes poorer.

figure 7.6 Growth poles

61

What often happens is that the growth pole has more links with the developed countries than with its hinterland. Overseas countries and companies therefore benefit more than the local people. This is shown in fig. 7.6B. The result is **dualism**. Contrasted levels of development exist side by side as illustrated in figs. 7.7 and 7.8. As a result of this process the wealthy **core** becomes richer while the poor **periphery** remains poor. In fact it may become even poorer than it was originally, as suggested in fig. 7.6B.

In Brazil, 75 per cent of manufacturing is located close to Rio de Janeiro and São Paulo. Figures 7.7 and 7.8 show how city-centre affluence can fade to surburban shanties and rural poverty. Sometimes the rural poverty is actually increased as in fig. 7.6B. If we think of the hoped-for wave of wealth and opportunities as the **swash**, we can understand the effect of '**backwash**' when rural products are drawn to the urban centres and the young people move to the 'perceived' opportunities in the cities (see Juan's story, p. 34).

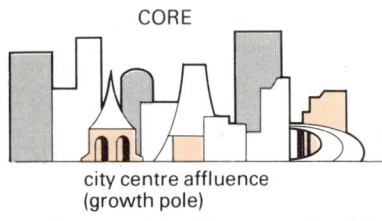 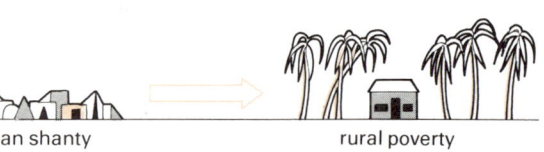

CORE

PERIPHERY

city centre affluence
(growth pole)

suburban shanty
towns

rural poverty

figure 7.7 Brazilian example of dualism

Because of the dangers of 'dualism' and 'backwash', many governments try to spread their economic growth throughout the country. They apply the philosophy that 'small is beautiful' as suggested by Dr E. Schumacher:

    cottage industries

    craft centres (weaving, pottery)

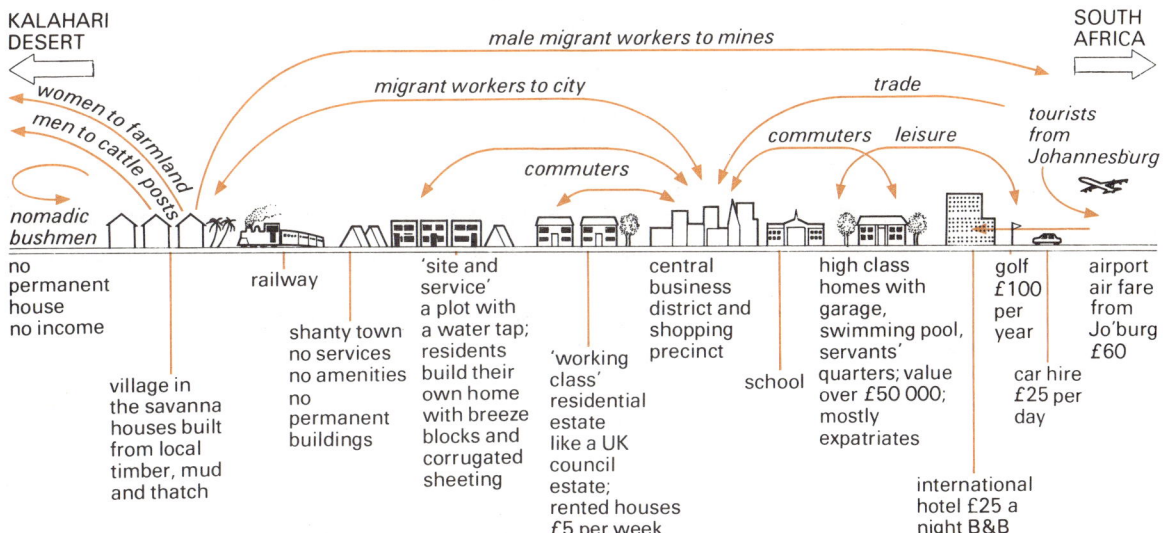

KALAHARI DESERT

male migrant workers to mines

SOUTH AFRICA

migrant workers to city

trade

women to farmland
men to cattle posts

commuters *leisure*

tourists from Johannesburg

commuters

nomadic bushmen

no permanent house no income

railway

shanty town no services no amenities no permanent buildings

'site and service' a plot with a water tap; residents build their own home with breeze blocks and corrugated sheeting

central business district and shopping precinct

school

high class homes with garage, swimming pool, servants' quarters; value over £50 000; mostly expatriates

golf £100 per year

car hire £25 per day

airport air fare from Jo'burg £60

village in the savanna houses built from local timber, mud and thatch

'working class' residential estate like a UK council estate; rented houses £5 per week

international hotel £25 a night B&B

figure 7.8 This transect across a third world growth pole shows a steep prosperity gradient. (Values are given in approximate UK sterling equivalent.)
It also shows the flow of people. What are the reasons for the movements of people?
(Based on observations of Gaborone, Botswana)

> comprehensive community schemes linking vocational, educational and commercial activities
> local agricultural advisory centres
> rural medical centres
> local production and training brigades.

These schemes are more likely to use **technology** that involves easily made and cheaply maintained machines, doing routine jobs such as carrying loads, pumping water, threshing grain and weaving cloth. They usually use manual, wind, animal or solar power so as to avoid dependence on the oil-producing nations. The technology employed in such schemes is carefully chosen to ensure it is **appropriate** to the situation in which it will be used.

figure 7.9 A modern steel plough being demonstrated by a World Bank agricultural adviser to a woman in Upper Volta

63

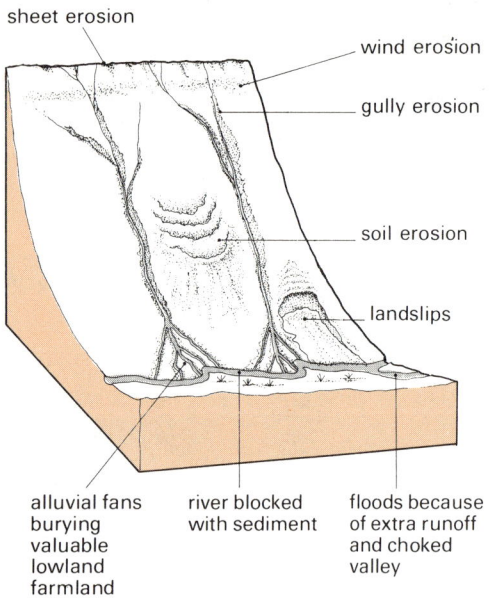

BEFORE RIVER CONTROL

sheet erosion

wind erosion

gully erosion

soil erosion

landslips

alluvial fans burying valuable lowland farmland

river blocked with sediment

floods because of extra runoff and choked valley

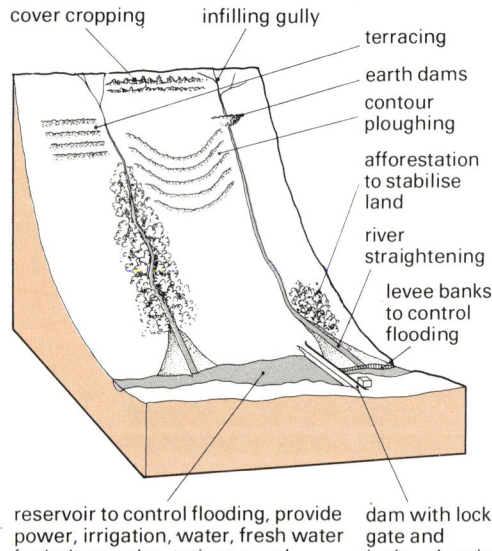

AFTER RIVER CONTROL

cover cropping

infilling gully

terracing

earth dams

contour ploughing

afforestation to stabilise land

river straightening

levee banks to control flooding

reservoir to control flooding, provide power, irrigation, water, fresh water for industry, domestic use and recreation, and to assist navigation

dam with lock gate and hydro-electric power station

figure 7.10 Development of river basins

Some nations reject the 'western' path toward material prosperity along with the pollution, stress, inflation, social and economic problems it can bring. They are keen to have a **centrally planned economy** as in communist countries:

public ownership of the means of production,

equal shares of profit,

incentives to productivity through exhortation (appeals) and commendation (praise) rather than cash or material benefit,

suppression of corruption, drunkenness, violence and vandalism,

housing, welfare and transport provided by the state,

full employment.

The USSR's five- or seven-year plans following the 1917 Revolution led to rapid growth of heavy industry and infrastructure but were accompanied by:

reduced availability of consumer goods,

low yields in agriculture,

a level of internal security and police vigilance which would be unacceptable in some countries.

Some development schemes have involved major projects which transform whole regions and modify the landscape and ecosystems. Some such schemes coincided with river basins. The model for these was the 1920s Tennessee Valley Authority Scheme. See fig. 7.10. Over the years the settlers from the east coast had cleared the forests for farming, causing soil erosion. The soil carried downriver choked the channel, causing floods. The whole valley became derelict. The TVA scheme was devised to develop the total resources of the whole valley in a coordinated programme:

soil conservation: contour ploughing, terracing, tree planting, gully filling, planting cover crops to prevent soil erosion and renovate damaged land.

dam building: to control flow and check flooding, provide reservoirs for fresh water, hydroelectric power (HEP), navigation and recreation.

industry was encouraged to exploit the new sources of power and transport facilities.

A derelict backwater became a prosperous agricultural and industrial area.

Similar schemes followed:

in Australia (Snowy River)

France (Rhone Valley)

Egypt (Aswan High Dam)

Ghana (Volta River).

Locate these schemes on a world map.

Such developments are not possible if the river is the boundary between hostile nations. In the case of the river Mekong, the riverside states of Thailand, Laos, Cambodia (now Kampuchea) and Vietnam have been in a state of war since 1940. In the case of the river Zambesi, the Kariba dam was planned jointly by North Rhodesia, South Rhodesia and Nyasaland which at that time formed a federation. Since then North Rhodesia and Nyasaland have become the independent states of Zambia and Malawi while Southern Rhodesia declared Unilateral Independence in 1965, remaining cut off from Zambia until it became independent Zimbabwe in 1979. As a result the Kariba Project never fulfilled its potential.

Summary

In this chapter the main ideas considered were:

- All countries are developing and always have been
- The way one country develops affects others
- There are many different types of development
- No one type of development is the 'ideal'
- There are many ways of measuring development
- Some types of development produce dualism
- Some types of development make the poor poorer
- Types of employment can be classified and ranked
- Development indicators can be graphed and mapped
- 'Small is beautiful'

Exercises

1   Make a list of the types of employment followed by your friends and relatives. Classify them into Primary, Secondary and Tertiary (see fig. 7.5). Convert them into percentages then rank them. What sort of pattern emerges?

2   Draw a copy of the transect across a third world growth pole shown in fig. 7.8.

Use the information provided in fig. 7.8 to draw a sketch graph of wealth against distance. First, draw the base line of the transect diagram again, labelling the different zones. This is the horizontal axis, representing distance. Add a vertical axis and label it low, medium and high wealth. For each zone, assess its level of wealth and mark this on the graph. Join up the points to form a graph. This is, in effect, a rough **prosperity profile**.

3   According to Rostow's model the UK is in the 'high consumption' stage. Write down all the evidence you can find in your own community to support this idea. Write a letter to a friend in an 'underdeveloped' country which is still in Rostow stage 1, giving him/her your comments on the advantages and disadvantages of 'Life in Stage 5'.

table 7.2 Number of patients per doctor (World Health Organisation statistics)

USSR	300
Sweden	580
USA	600
France	650
Uruguay	700
UK	750
Libya	1 020
Egypt	1 190
Brazil	1 650
Bolivia	2 120
India	3 960
Ghana	11 420
Haiti	11 170
Ethiopia	84 350
Tanzania	18 490
Malawi	48 500
Upper Volta	56 480

4 Plot the NUMBER OF PATIENTS PER DOCTOR figures in table 7.2 on a graph like fig. 6.11 with latitude on the horizontal axis. What pattern emerges? Compare them with any other measures of well-being available to you (there are quite a few in various parts of this book).

5 Invent for each of the following a piece of appropriate technology which would be useful in a remote community in an underdeveloped country.
(a) A means of raising water from a well 15 m deep.
(b) A means of storing water from the rainy season through the dry season.
(c) Transport for village craft-products to market 20 km away without use of cars, trucks or animals.
Try to outline the criteria you use in the exercise.

6 Describe how 'rivers may divide but valleys unite'. See fig. 7.11.

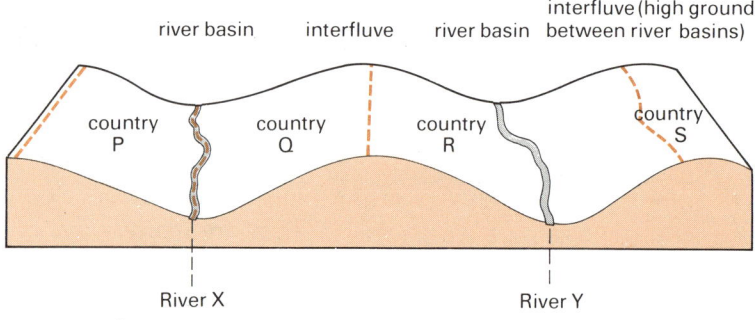

figure 7.11 River basins and national frontiers

7 What do you understand by the word *infrastructure*?

8 'Ten thousand people die each day from lack of nourishment and 500 million are regularly undernourished. It would take 12 million tonnes of grain a year to feed the starving. In 1974, 373 million tonnes of grain were used by developed countries for animal feed.'
Comment on this statement.

9 Figure 7.8 shows people moving for a variety of reasons. Make a table like fig. 4.8 and enter the different types of movement shown in fig. 7.8.

8 Regional differences in development

Figure 8.1 shows a European upland region with dairy/sheep farms and villages round the edges. It is drained by streams radiating from a central granite highland.

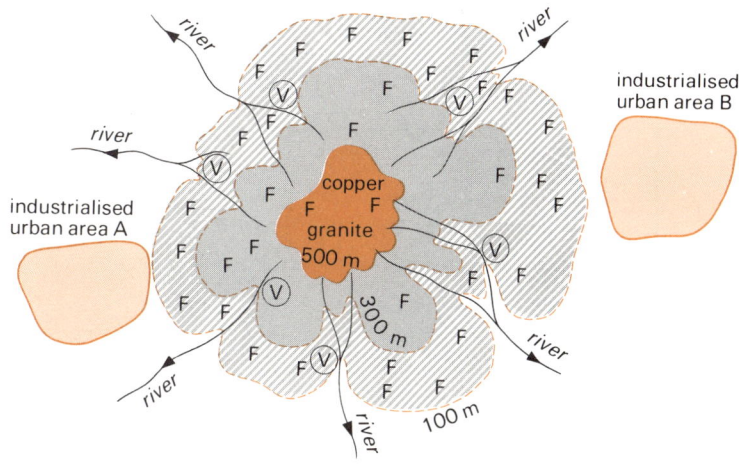

figure 8.1 A European upland with peripheral dairy/sheep farms and villages

F farm
(V) village
heights given in metres

Draw a circle 10 cm diameter to represent this upland. Draw in it some farms F , villages (v) and streams. Join the farms to the villages with tracks and the villages to the lowlands with roads —— . Dam two streams to produce reservoirs . Plant forests on the higher ridges. Quarry the granite and mine the copper in the central highlands. Put a motorway through the middle to link the bordering industrial lowlands A and B. Abandon any high remote farms . Build a hostel for tourists in the central highlands.

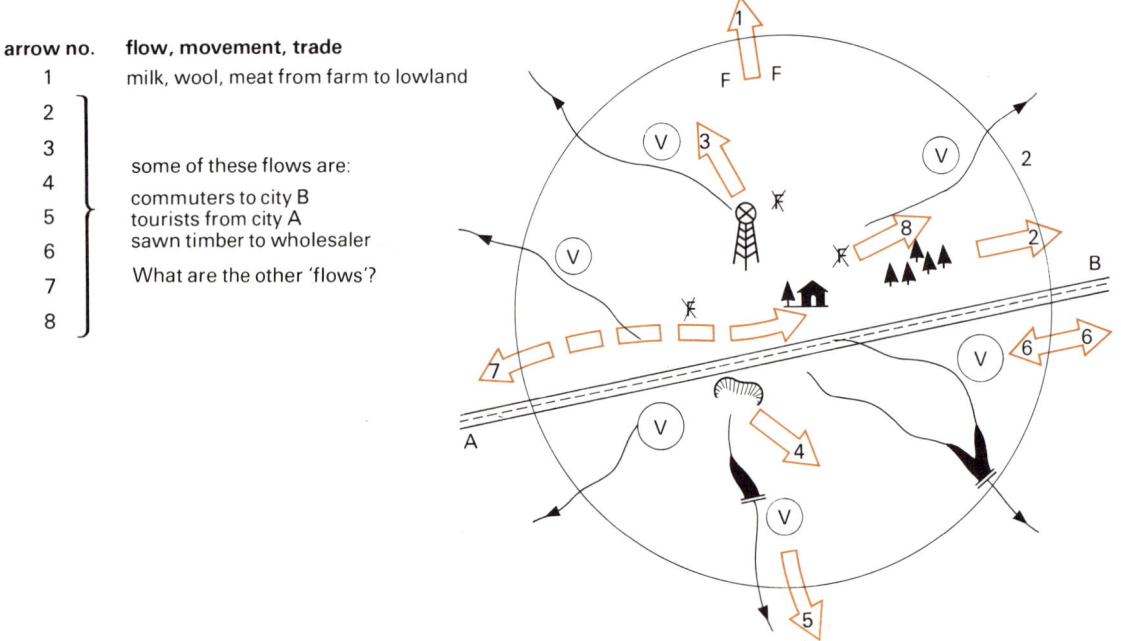

arrow no.	flow, movement, trade
1	milk, wool, meat from farm to lowland
2	
3	some of these flows are:
4	commuters to city B
5	tourists from city A
6	sawn timber to wholesaler
7	What are the other 'flows'?
8	

figure 8.2 Development of a European upland

This region has become an area of 'outflow' with resources moving to the adjacent lowlands: water, timber, milk, meat and minerals all 'flow' down to the lowlands. When depopulation begins, the labour force also flows down to the industrial towns. The tidal flow of people *daily* (the commuters), at *weekends* (trippers) and *seasonally* (tourists) are in effect the 'export' of scenery.

These ideas can be applied to North East England. Figures 8.3 and 8.4 show the movements of people and resources from North West Northumberland towards Teesside. Similar effects can be seen if Greater Glasgow is linked with the Scottish Highlands, or the West Midlands with Mid Wales. Draw a diagram like fig. 8.3 to illustrate the movements of people and resources in one of these two examples.

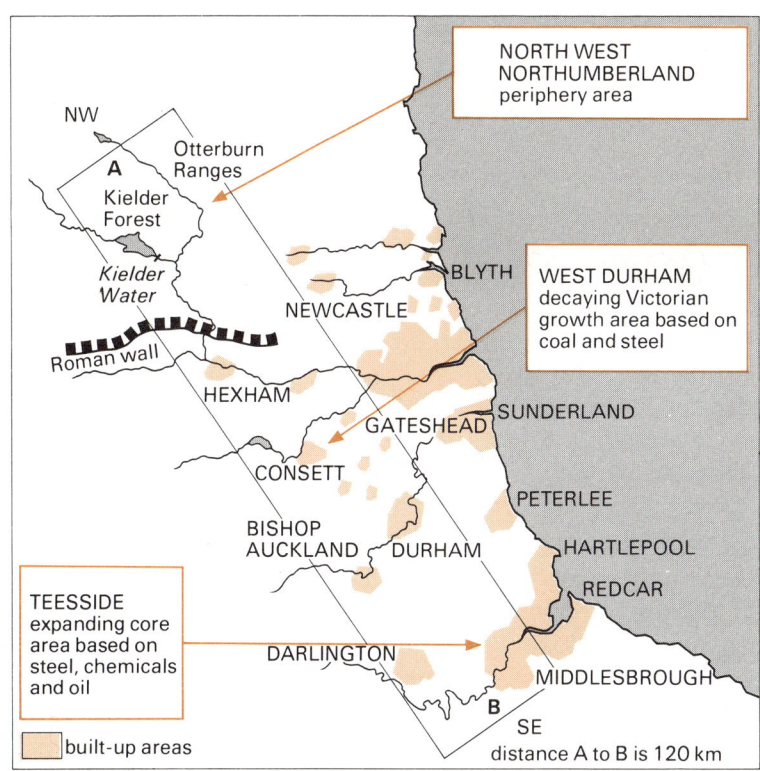

figure 8.3 The core/periphery concept as applied to a section of North East England

NORTH WEST NORTHUMBERLAND periphery area

WEST DURHAM decaying Victorian growth area based on coal and steel

NW

Otterburn Ranges

A

Kielder Forest

Kielder Water

Roman wall

NEWCASTLE

BLYTH

HEXHAM

GATESHEAD

SUNDERLAND

CONSETT

PETERLEE

BISHOP AUCKLAND

DURHAM

HARTLEPOOL

REDCAR

DARLINGTON

MIDDLESBROUGH

SE

B

distance A to B is 120 km

TEESSIDE expanding core area based on steel, chemicals and oil

built-up areas

figure 8.4 Movements of people and resources from North West Northumberland to Teesside

Can you suggest what captions should be inserted on the unmarked arrows pointing in the reverse direction?

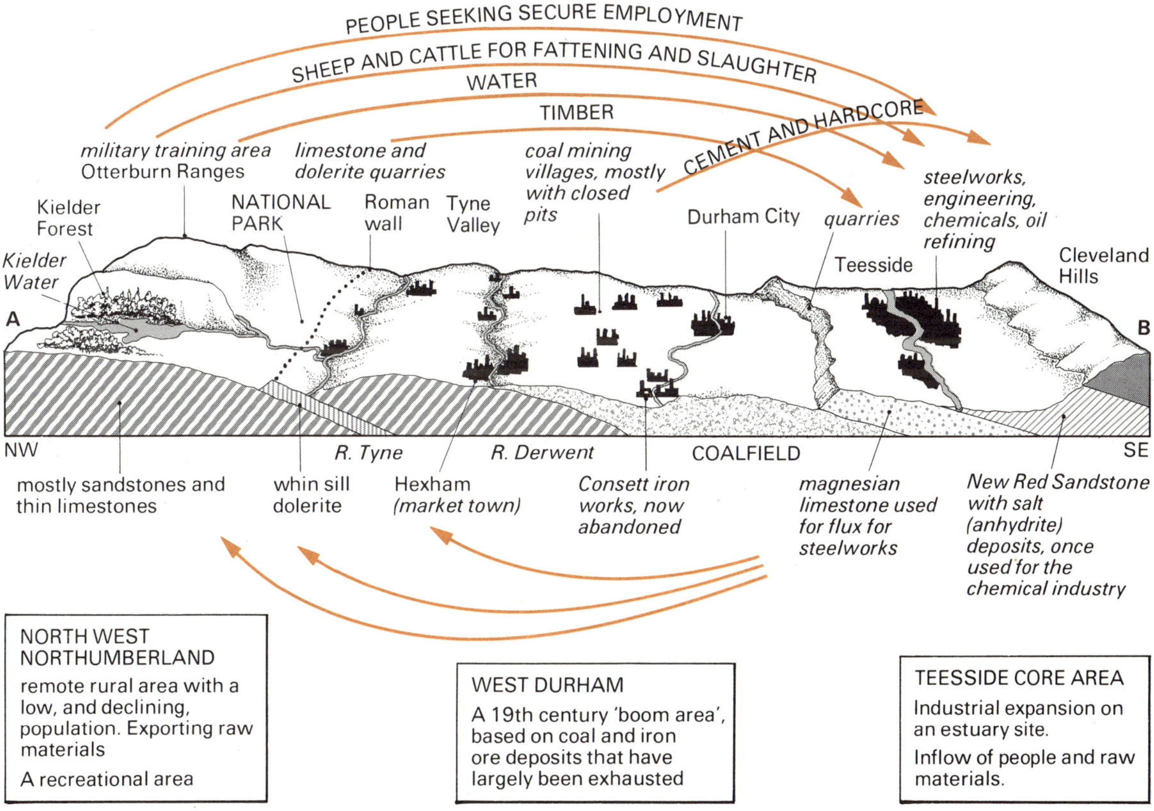

PEOPLE SEEKING SECURE EMPLOYMENT

SHEEP AND CATTLE FOR FATTENING AND SLAUGHTER

WATER

TIMBER

CEMENT AND HARDCORE

military training area Otterburn Ranges

limestone and dolerite quarries

Roman wall Tyne Valley

coal mining villages, mostly with closed pits

Durham City *quarries*

steelworks, engineering, chemicals, oil refining

Kielder Forest

NATIONAL PARK

Teesside

Cleveland Hills

Kielder Water

A

B

NW

SE

R. Tyne   *R. Derwent*   COALFIELD

mostly sandstones and thin limestones

whin sill dolerite

Hexham *(market town)*

Consett iron works, now abandoned

magnesian limestone used for flux for steelworks

New Red Sandstone with salt (anhydrite) deposits, once used for the chemical industry

NORTH WEST NORTHUMBERLAND

remote rural area with a low, and declining, population. Exporting raw materials

A recreational area

WEST DURHAM

A 19th century 'boom area', based on coal and iron ore deposits that have largely been exhausted

TEESSIDE CORE AREA

Industrial expansion on an estuary site.

Inflow of people and raw materials.

Fig. 8.5A shows the tropical coast of the former colony of a West European state.

> Make a copy of the map in fig. 8.5A.
>
> Place a port (P) on the estuary and lay a railway +++ to extract the timber from the southern forest. Plant rubber trees on the south-east coast. Sink a tin mine in the western highlands and a bauxite quarry in the far north. Link them all to the port with roads —— and a bridge. Build a tourist resort R on the coast. Show the flow of resources ——► and tourists ◄--► .

In fig. 8.5B we show the metropolitan core of a European state. Compare it with:
(a) the distant tropical coast of its former colony (fig. 8.5A)
(b) the upland region in its hinterland (see figs. 8.1 and 8.2)

These models suggest that patterns of development vary from region to region. Some areas can be thought of as **core** regions attracting trade and industry, thus accumulating great wealth. Other regions are on the **periphery** of the same economic systems, experiencing an outflow of resources, manpower and wealth.

Before going any further, make a note of some of the reasons why different regions may follow contrasted development paths.

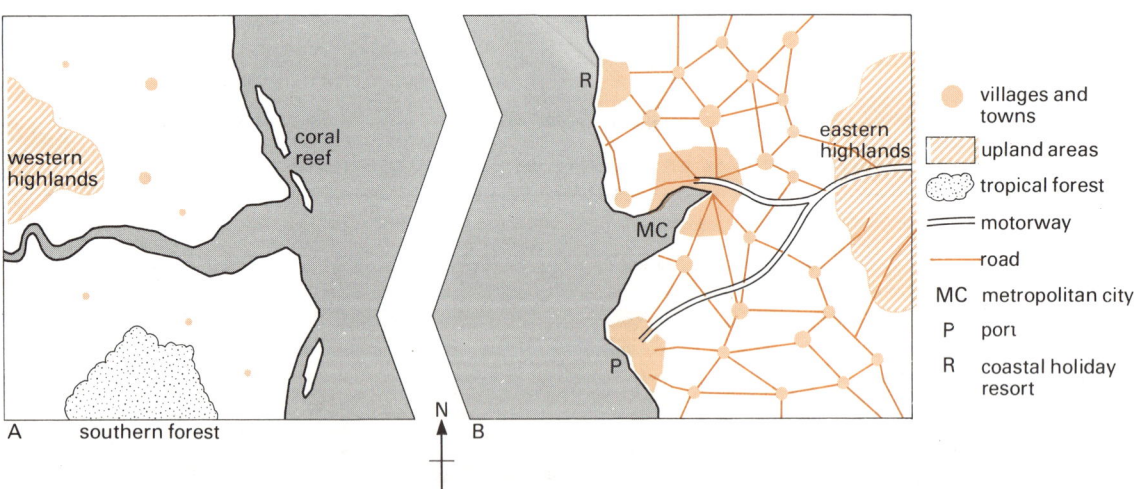

figure 8.5 Contrasting developments of estuaries

Some of the reasons you have just noted may appear in this checklist:

> **REASONS FOR CONTRASTS IN DEVELOPMENT MAY INCLUDE:**
>
> 1. Natural advantages of climate, soils, position
> 2. Resource endowment
> 3. Population distribution and structure
> 4. Technological capacities
> 5. Access to world trade routes
> 6. History
> 7. Relations with neighbouring states
> 8. Political stability
> 9. Patterns of land tenure and internal government

We shall now consider these reasons for contrast in some detail.

1 Differences in natural advantages

Figure 8.6 suggests some of the reasons why areas can be **inhospitable** or difficult to develop. Make a list of environments which are unfavourable for economic growth and which have a low natural potential. You could use this table as a guide.

Try to identify on fig. 8.6 the positions of the photographs on pages 73-5. Locate on a world map each of the countries mentioned in the photograph captions.

Negative or inhospitable environments	Reasons why these environments are difficult to develop
Ice caps	Extreme cold; frozen soil; remote; communications difficult.
Marshlands etc.	

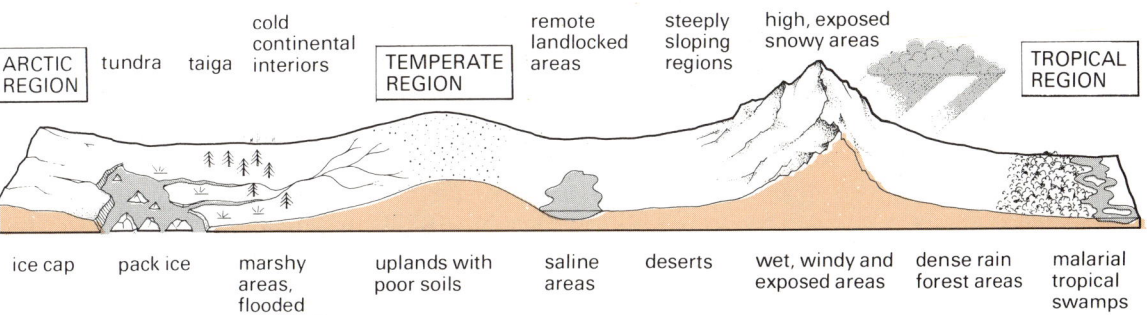

figure 8.6 Transect across the northern hemisphere, showing natural environments

Even these unfavoured regions could develop if there was a strong enough incentive to start activities such as *mining*, *tourism* or *strategic defence*. Use your atlas to add to the examples in this table

Economic activity	Example of an inhospitable place developed for the activity
Oil mining	North slope of Alaska ...
Winter sports etc.	

Now suggest where the world's most favoured environments are to be found. If you plot them on a world map you could describe the pattern which emerges. Try to relate it to altitude, latitude, relief, climate, etc.

2 Differences in resource endowment

Some countries are fortunate in having a wide enough range of food production, energy sources and industrial raw materials to be almost **self-sufficient**. Others have become dependent on the export or processing of resources vital to the economies of the industrialised nations. Copy table 8.1 and complete column B by matching each resource to one of these countries: Iceland, Sri Lanka, Saudi Arabia, Gambia, Ghana, Guyana, Finland, Malaysia.

A number of world organisations exist to try to control the production and price of certain *key commodities*.

WORLD TRADE ORGANISATIONS attempting to control production and price of key resources include:

GATT, *The General Agreement on Trade and Tariffs*, is a group of politicians and industrialists from the developed world, trying to reduce the tariffs on goods bought from the third world. Talks take place in a series of 'rounds', e.g. the 'Kennedy Round' and the 'Tokyo Round'.

CIEC, *The Conference on International Economic Co-operation*, (the North-South Dialogue), considers the world energy crisis but is blocked by the wish of OPEC for other commodity prices to be included. (See page 81 for explanation of OPEC.)

Lomé Convention An agreement between the EEC countries

table 8.1

A Resource	B Country dependent on export/ processing
ground nuts cocoa tin oil fish tea timber bauxite	

and their former colonies offers to the former colonies (a) preferential entry into European markets and (b) stable prices. (See page 81 for explanation of EEC.)

UNCTAD, *The United Nations Conference on Trade and Development*, is held every four years to review world commodity prices. Results are often deadlocked by the conflict between the poorer countries' desire to get more for their commodities and the rich countries' desire for cheap raw materials.

Efforts to agree on world commodity prices have met with little success. But most parties agree on the need for a common fund to pay for 'buffer stocks'. These 'buffer stocks' are used to cushion both producers and consumers against any fluctuations in supply and demand.

Some of the most important **core commodities** and the leading producers include:

COCOA	Ghana (31%), Nigeria (20%), Ivory Coast (12%).
COFFEE	Brazil (27%), Colombia (12%), Uganda (12%).
TEA	Sri Lanka (32%), India (32%), Kenya (7%).
RUBBER	Malaysia (47%), Indonesia (27%), Thailand (11%).
TIN	Malaysia (43%), Bolivia (14%), Thailand (10%).
JUTE	India (42%), Bangladesh (34%).
BANANAS	Ecuador (20%), Honduras (17%), Costa Rica (13%).

3 Population distribution

In some regions economic development has been handicapped by a shortage of labour. In other regions development is hindered by overcrowding. Suggest how under- or overpopulation has affected the economic growth of these regions and countries:

Alaska, Bangladesh, Turkey, Western Australia, Siberia.

How can countries overcome the problem of *overemployment* (too many jobs available for the size of the population as in Iceland)? Your answer may include people who do several jobs, additional work being done by mothers, children and old people, and extra labour from guest workers and immigrants.

How can countries tackle the problem of *underemployment* (too few jobs for the size of the population as in Ireland)? Try to structure your answer to draw out the opposite effects from those in overemployment situations.

Sedentary subsistence cultivation – garlic growing, India

4 Different technological capacities

These can be expressed in a diagram:

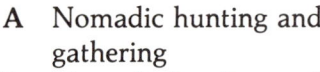

INCREASING LEVELS OF TECHNOLOGY IN FOOD PRODUCTION

- **A** Nomadic hunting and gathering
- **B** Nomadic herding and cultivating
- **C** Sedentary subsistence cultivation
- **D** Commercial extensive grazing
- **E** Commercial extensive cereal growing
- **F** Commercial plantation agriculture
- **G** Intensive mixed farming
- **H** Horticulture and fruit farming
- **I** Factory farming with artificial environments and scientifically balanced feeding

Commercial grazing – Iceland

Nomadic herding – Saudi Arabia

Extensive commercial cereal growing – USSR

You can see how these levels of technology relate to the transport and infrastructure models in fig. 7.5.

Types A, B and C are characteristic of less developed countries.

Types D to H may be organised as individual or cooperative or collective enterprises.

Types F, H and I may be sometimes owned by a major company involved with marketing foods or vegetable products (such as fibres, oils or rubber).

For this photograph of cattle farming in Niger, make up a title using words introduced in this section of the chapter.

GLOSSARY

nomadic Moving as a family, village or tribe from one location to another in search of food or new pastures. Largely confined to the 'wilderness' areas of the world's desert, mountain, rainforest and tundra regions.

sedentary Remaining in one location. Ownership of the land may be in the hands of the family, village or a landlord.

extensive A low level of labour and/or capital per unit area.

intensive A high level of labour and/or capital investment per unit area.

subsistence Producing food for consumption by the family or village, any occasional surplus being traded for essential clothing or equipment.

commercial The production of crops or animals for sale.

One of the most effective ways of helping developing countries to increase food supplies has been to apply modern technology to the traditional farming systems as in B, C and D. This has been called the **green revolution** and involves

applying fertilisers   demonstration farms
draining swampland   agricultural loans
irrigating dry land   scientific breeding
simple mechanisation   better crop storage
High Yielding Varieties (HYVs) of crops

In 1977, 30% of the ricelands of South East Asia were under HYVs

20% of the Chinese riceland and 25% of its wheatlands were under HYVs.

Clearly one of the most important options open to any third world country is to upgrade its agriculture in this manner.

5 Access to world trade routes

Over 90 per cent of world shipping enters or leaves industrial countries of Western Europe, North America, Australia and Japan. Raw materials (especially oil, minerals and chemicals) and large manufactured goods (such as cars, machinery) are being shipped in increasing quantities. High value/low bulk products are now commonly moved by air.

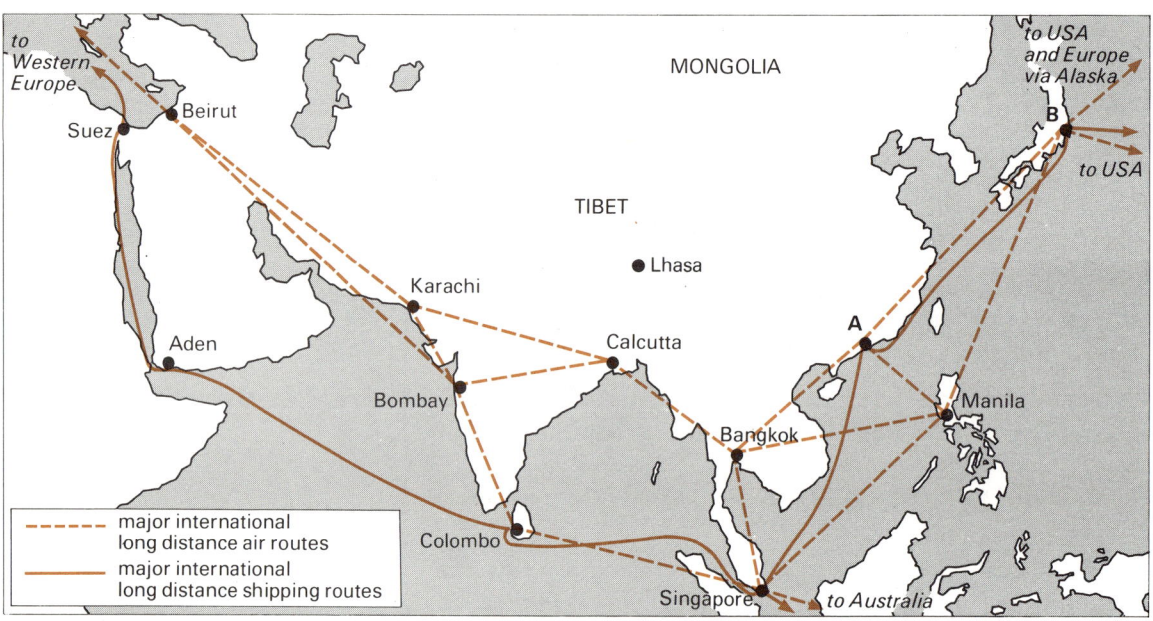

figure 8.7 Asia: routeways

Figure 8.7 shows how some cities lying at the intersection of major air and sea routes have become nodal points for trade and commerce. The map also shows the remote location of places such as Tibet and Mongolia. Could you locate similar nodal points and isolated areas in South America and Africa?

Figure 8.8 suggests the economic core and the remote periphery regions of Western Europe. Attempt to explain why the core region includes South East England, the Benelux countries, the North Rhine lowlands, the Paris Basin and North Italy.

Name as many of the periphery regions as possible. Suggest reasons why some regions may in the future become less or more peripheral.

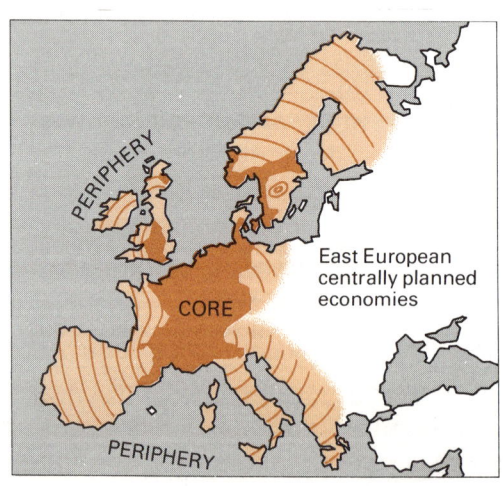

figure 8.8 Europe: core and periphery

6 Different histories

Each nation of the world has its own individual history. But it is possible to see general patterns of historical development.

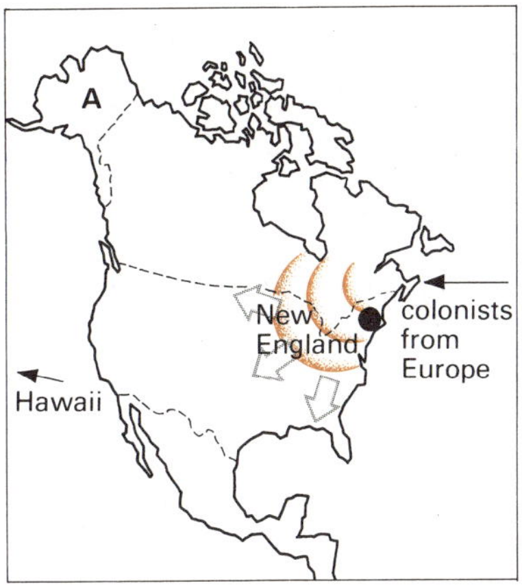

A. The 'superpowers'

Both of the world's 'superpowers' have a well established nucleus from which new development has spread in a 'frontier' style of colonisation. The USA grew from the eastern seaboard westward into the Prairies and across the Rockies to the Pacific coast. The USSR grew from the Russian Heartland (the Leningrad–Moscow–Kiev region) eastwards into Siberia and across to the Pacific coast. Despite their contrasting political systems, both have absorbed new territories, peoples and resources. They have become economically strong technological states, ringed by nuclear defence systems and orbiting satellites.

figure 8.9 The USA was settled by colonisation from the eastern seaboard

What aboriginal people were in the way of the frontiersmen? What is state A, and how did the USA acquire it?

B. Western European countries

Between the sixteenth and twentieth centuries many West European states brought a collection of colonies under their control. The first empire-builders were Britain, France, Belgium, Spain, Portugal and the Netherlands. Germany and Italy did not become unified nations until the late nineteenth century and so were much later in acquiring colonies.

The development of these states and their colonies was strongly influenced by this imperialist phase. When most colonies won independence after World War II, the former imperialists' economies (the British, Belgian and Portugese especially) were weakened as they lost their cheap sources of raw materials and their guaranteed markets. Now that the former colonies are industrialising, they are threatening the markets of their former masters.

Some of Europe's most wealthy nations (such as Sweden and Switzerland) were never colonial powers. Their histories have been characterised by neutrality.

C. The European communist satellites

The partition of Europe by the 'Iron Curtain' after 1945 produced a new group of communist countries. Except for Albania and Yugoslavia they came under the influence of the USSR. All these states have centrally planned economies as described on page 64.

D. The frontier countries

When settlers from 'advanced' countries arrive in an empty 'wilderness' they do not, as a rule, begin a systematic and

77

planned pattern of settlement. They exploit the most accessible sources of wealth, land, animals, timber and energy first. Only as more people move in to settle, and an infrastructure develops, does the pioneer fringe give way to controlled land use and resource development. The 'frontier' environment still survives in Canada, Australia, Iceland and Brazil.

E. South East Asia monsoon lands

Most of the countries of South East Asia are still characterised by the intensive farming of small plots by peasant farmers. Here, over half the world's people live on 15 per cent of the earth's surface. The whole region has been deeply affected by land ownership struggles, by strict religious discipline and by contact with colonial powers such as Britain, France, Netherlands and (more recently) Japan.

F. Industrialised Far East

Japan has industrialised so rapidly this century that by 1980 it had outstripped the rest of the world in automobile production. There was similar growth in electronics, ship building and optics. Meanwhile, Korea, Hong Kong, Taiwan and Malaysia have embarked on similar development paths.

G. Latin American countries

The Latin American countries became independent from European colonial power quite early, following a history of slave-worked plantation economies. Their unnatural growth led to political instability which has held back development. Localised **core** areas of extreme prosperity (as in Venezuela and south-east Brazil) lie alongside backward peripheral areas with very low growth rates. This contrast contributes to political instability.

H. 'Emerging' ex-colonial African states

Most ex-colonial 'new' countries are in low latitudes and are 'less developed countries' with low GNP per capita. (See page 48). Many retain links with their former colonial masters through such organisations as the Commonwealth. Their development remains closely tied to the economies of Western Europe.

I. Oil-exporting states

Since the grouping of these states into OPEC (the Organisation of Petroleum Exporting Countries), an important and powerful new world force has emerged. These states have accumulated vast reserves of wealth. Their oil price increases have encouraged international inflation. Some of their reserves of 'petrodollars' are now being used to assist the development of third world countries. Surprisingly, some of the oil states are themselves relatively underdeveloped despite their high GNP per capita. (See fig. 6.7.)

J. Political isolates

Both Israel and South Africa have had to develop in isolation because of the hostility of their neighbours. Israel is forced to devote a large part of its GNP to its defence forces. South Africa's **apartheid** policies have alienated world opinion and have forced it, by trade embargoes, to strive for self-sufficiency. Deprived of sufficient oil imports, South Africa had to evolve the South African Synthetic Oil (SASOL) plant to make expensive oil from its own coal deposits.

This attempt to classify countries according to the way their histories have influenced their development is valuable in describing broad patterns. However, it may give an over-simplified picture. By now, you should be in the habit of checking the views of others, in your own reading, viewing and discussions.

7   Relationships with neighbouring states

The history of Israel, South Africa, Ireland and East Africa shows how hostility between neighbours can hinder development. On the other hand, it is possible for states to reach agreements with neighbours sharing common interests such as trade, currency exchange rates or joint development projects. Some industries, like aerospace, are now too costly for individual states to support. Concorde and the expensive satellite progammes are examples of international collaboration.

8   Political stability

A period of war or social unrest is often seen to disrupt a country's development. You can find evidence of this by collecting cuttings from current newspaper reports of terrorist activities, armed coups, border wars, etc. Over and above the material damage and loss of life, there is a permanent drain of wealth into arms spending, even in those nations which are apparently at peace.

You will find all the organisations listed in table 8.2 (p. 81) mentioned at various times in the press.

In some states, like Kampuchea (formerly Cambodia), Vietnam, Uganda and Ethiopia, warfare has severely damaged industry and infrastructure. Can you predict how huge population losses may have long-term effects on future development?

Represent this information on a world map:

SERIOUS ARMED CONFLICTS SINCE 1960

EUROPE Cyprus (civil war 1963–67), Northern Ireland (1968–), Portugal (military coup 1974), Cyprus (Turkish/Greek war 1974–76), Spain (Basque Separatists).

AFRICA Zaire (Katanga war 1960–66), Angola (War of Independence 1961–76), Morocco/Algeria (Border wars 1963–64), Mozambique (War of liberation 1965–75), Nigeria (Biafran war 1967–70), Ethiopia (Eritrean war 1969–79), Chad (civil war 1970–80), Burundi (massacre of Hutus 1972), Egypt/Libya (border war 1979), Uganda (Tanzanian-backed coup 1979), Zimbabwe (guerilla war 1978–79), Western Sahara (war 1976–).

MIDDLE EAST Iraq (civil war vs Kurds 1960–70), Yemen (civil war 1962–), Israel (3rd Arab–Israel war 1967–73), Lebanon (civil war 1970s, 1980s), Iran (revolution 1977–79), Iraq/Iran war (1980–).

ASIA Vietnam (major war involving 1.8 million deaths 1960–75), China/Indo-China (border war 1962), India/Pakistan (border war 1965–66), Indonesia (civil war 1965), USSR/China (border war 1969), Pakistan (E. Pakistan became Bangladesh 1971).

NORTH AND SOUTH AMERICA Cuba (missile crisis 1962), El Salvador/Honduras (border war 1969), Chile (coup 1973), Argentina (military coup 1976), Nicaragua (civil war 1979), El Salvador (civil war 1980–   ).

Try to keep this information up to date.

9 Land tenure and internal government

The whole direction and speed of development in a country can alter suddenly after a change of government. Though it is dangerous to generalise in this field, *right wing* governments tend to encourage individual ownership and private enterprise while *left wing* governments tend to favour public ownership of land and the means of production.

table 8.2

Organisation	Number of member countries in 1978	Date of formation	Members/Purpose
Commonwealth	37	1949	Former British colonies/dominions; trade
Organisation for Economic Cooperation and Development (OECD)	25	1961	To promote third world development by 'western' developed nations
North Atlantic Treaty Organisation (NATO)	18	1948	USA and Western Europe; defence alliance
European Economic Community (EEC)	10 + 2	1958	The 9 members of the West European Common Market, with the recent addition of Greece and likely addition of Spain and Portugal
European Free Trade Association (EFTA)	6	1960	Austria, Iceland, Norway, Portugal, Sweden and Switzerland; free trade alliance
Council for Mutual Economic Assistance (CMEA or COMECON)	9	1948	Communist 'common market', with other associate members such as Laos, N. Korea, Angola, Vietnam, Yugoslavia
Colombo Plan	21	1951	Limited technical cooperation and aid in SE Asia
Association of South East Asian Nations (ASEAN)	5	1967	Cooperation between Indonesia, Malaysia, Philippines and Thailand
Central Treaty Organisation (CENTO)	6	1955	Defence and trade agreements with USA, UK and Turkey, Iran, Iraq and Pakistan to defend USSR borders
Organisation of American States (OAS)	26	1948	North & South American countries conference, with programme to support economic and social development
Latin American Free Trade Association (LAFTA)	10	1961	Trade agreements
Central American Common Market (ODECA)	5	1960	El Salvador, Guatemala, Honduras, Nicaragua, Costa Rica
Caribbean Community (CARICOM)	13	1973	A common market agreement for Caribbean countries
Arab League	20	1945	A league to foster cooperation with common market status after 1973
East African Community	3	1961	Kenya, Tanzania, Uganda, finally broke up in 1978 as a result of different political policies of 3 countries
Organisation of African Unity (OAU)	30 +	1963	To foster African cooperation, and to eliminate colonialism
Organisation of Oil Producing Countries (OPEC)	13	1973	To determine the market value of crude oil.

Summary

The following sentences sum up the main ideas that have been covered in this chapter:

- Some countries have natural advantages of climate, soil, minerals or location
- Contrasts in development are explained by a number of different features
- Countries can co-operate to their mutual advantage
- Some countries and regions are remote and isolated, others are at nodal points
- Traditional cultures are often threatened by 'development'
- Mineral wealth or strategic position can develop even remote countries

Exercises

1   PENNINES   WELSH UPLAND   VOSGES
SCOTTISH HIGHLANDS   APPALACHIANS

Find out more from references about any three of these regions.
(a) Draw a diagram similar to fig. 8.2 to represent the pattern of development of each region.
(b) Write comments on the way each has developed.
How does your diagram compare with the model in fig. 8.2?

2 Copy the table of increasing levels of technology in food production on page 74. Alongside each level print examples, including the following:

     Canadian Prairie wheat farming
     Argentine Pampas beef production
     Ivory Coast palm oil production
     Kalahari Desert Bushman
     Danish dairy/pig/arable farm
     South of France vineyard.

3 Parts of East Africa have been designated Wildlife Conservation Areas. Some of this land is also needed for cattle grazing and subsistence cultivation. What evidence would you collect and what arguments would you submit in order to support the statement
either that the land should be used to feed humans rather than to preserve endangered plants and animal species,
or that the land should be set aside for a permanent sanctuary for wildlife at the expense of human hunger.

4 Table 8.3 shows the percentages of the world production of certain commodities which come from third world countries.
What would be the result if the producers grouped together like OPEC?

5 Monitor TV and radio broadcasts for a week and list all the international organisations mentioned (e.g. NATO, EEC). When you have a list add to each organisation the names of its members and its purpose. Draw a Venn diagram to show which countries belong in which sets. Comment on the result.

table 8.3 Percentage of commodities produced by third world countries

cocoa	100
rubber	99.9
coffee	99.8
hard fibres	98.5
jute	88.7
tin	75.0
tea	68.8
rice	56.0
bauxite	48.8
cotton	44.6
copper	37.6

6 Turn back to the list of reasons for contrasted development which you constructed (see page 70). Make any amendments you now think necessary.

7 Draw a world map to represent the information in the section on 'different histories' (page 77).

8 Figure 8.8 shows the core regions of Europe. Draw a map to show the core regions and the 'peripheral' regions of either Europe or North America or Africa. Add to your map other information and comments which help explain the importance of the core regions and the lack of development of the peripheral regions.

9 Figure 8.7 shows nodal growth points. What are the cities A and B? Compare Singapore with Lhasa in terms of nodality.

10 A lot of goods are manufactured in the Far East, often by large multinational corporations. Show as many as you can in a table like this:

Article	Country of manufacture	Manufacturing company
TV set	Japan	Sony

Repeat this exercise for goods from third world countries.

9 Examples of development in practice

When we are looking for common patterns we use models to help our understanding. But the models may oversimplify the detail and the individuality of the real life examples we are studying. In this chapter we select a variety of real examples and examine their recent development patterns.

Each of the countries has a distinctive mix of problems. There is no single cure (such as industrialisation, population control or a 'green revolution') for the problems.

Ghana

The British colony of the Gold Coast became independent under its first president, Dr Nkrumah, in 1957. It was a country of great potential and it promised to become a model for the development of many emerging African nations.

Apart from the agricultural resources of its southern rain forests, Ghana had reserves of gold, diamonds, bauxite, chrome, iron ore and some petroleum. What it lacked was the infrastructure necessary to exploit these resources. Except at Takoradi, cargoes had to be offloaded on to small, hand-paddled surf boats in rough seas. The roads, railways, power and water resources were similarly inadequate to support modernisation. President Nkrumah launched a bold plan to develop the country on Rostow-type lines (see page 60).

A huge dam built across the river Volta at Akosombo flooded 3 per cent of the country, creating Africa's largest man-made lake, Lake Volta. The hydro-electric power (HEP) generated from this dam could more than satisfy domestic needs, leaving a surplus for export to neighbouring states. Bauxite from the Ashanti hills and Awaso was reduced to alumina and smelted to aluminium using this new cheap HEP. The cost of this TVA style project (see page 64) was over $300 million. In addition, there was the expense of moving the farmers to higher ground, building the power station, roads, rail and transmission lines, smelters and the new port at Tema. At the same time the food processing, textile and engineering industries were developed and a prestige national airline was established.

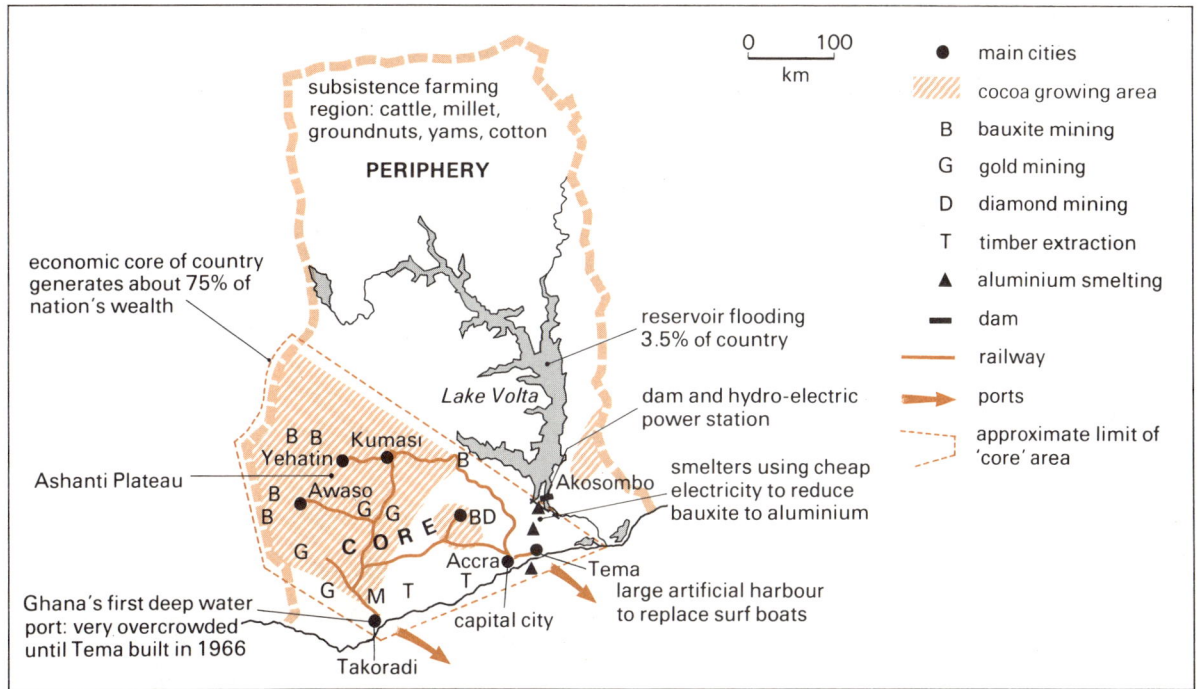

figure 9.1 Ghana

The map shows:

- scale: 0 — 100 km
- **main cities** ●
- **cocoa growing area** (hatched)
- **B** bauxite mining
- **G** gold mining
- **D** diamond mining
- **T** timber extraction
- ▲ aluminium smelting
- **—** dam
- railway
- **→** ports
- approximate limit of 'core' area

subsistence farming region: cattle, millet, groundnuts, yams, cotton

PERIPHERY

economic core of country generates about 75% of nation's wealth

reservoir flooding 3.5% of country

dam and hydro-electric power station

Lake Volta

smelters using cheap electricity to reduce bauxite to aluminium

Ashanti Plateau

Yehatin Kumasi B B B

Awaso B

G G **CORE** BD

G M T

Accra T

Tema

large artificial harbour to replace surf boats

Akosombo

capital city

Ghana's first deep water port: very overcrowded until Tema built in 1966

Takoradi

Akosombo Dam, Ghana

Using modern equipment to remove hardwood trees from a forest in southern Ghana

The country ran into severe debt financing all these improvements. It still depended too much on the sale of commodities which were subject to world market fluctuations. The native agriculture had not been developed enough to support industrialisation. There was a serious lack of skilled technicians.

So Ghana had built up an impressive infrastructure — and a severe debt. Its extravagant 'Rolls Royce' style of development has not been copied by other emerging nations.

Jamaica

The Caribbean became 'the sugar bowl of Europe' in these stages:

1. The native Caribs were eradicated by European settlers.
2. African slaves were shipped in as cheap labour.
3. Plantations were established as one of the 'corners' of the 'triangle trade'.

The profits from this eighteenth-century trade helped to finance Britain's Industrial Revolution.

The Triangle Trade

Name the countries at the vertices of the triangle.

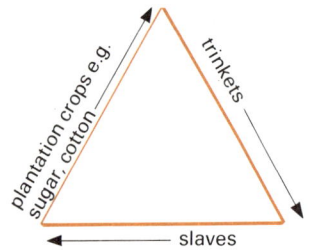

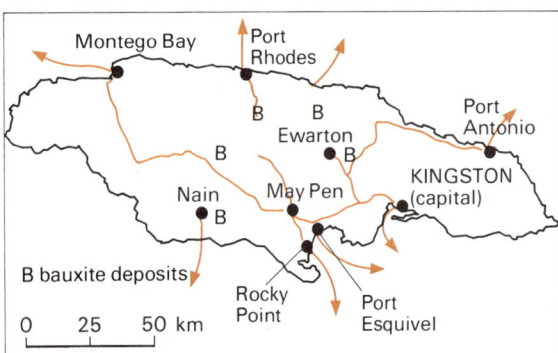

figure 9.2 Jamaica

Draw a small sketch map of the Caribbean region to show the position of Jamaica in relation to the USA, Cuba and the Tropic of Cancer.

Sugar harvesting in Jamaica

But in the early nineteenth century the trade suffered competition from other sugar producers. The end of the system of slavery meant that labour had to be hired from India and China, thereby increasing the racial mix of the Caribbean area. It follows that islands like Jamaica experienced no steady evolution of population, culture and economy. They grew as 'manufactured societies, labour camps, the creations of Empire' (V. S. Naipaul). Their economies were over-dependent on sugar.

In addition to sugar, Jamaica today relies on bauxite and tourism as its major sources of wealth. The bauxite is in the hands of large multinational companies. The tourism is subject to changing fashions and the state of the world economy. Secondary (manufacturing) industry accounts for only 10 per cent of exports. Much of the nation's food has to be imported. Agriculture is mostly in the hands of peasants, who are under-mechanised and poorly placed to supply the food needs of the country.

The recent rapid population increase provided a cheap supply of labour for 'screwdriver' style industries which required little skill. This led to 'Industrialisation by Invitation'. Manufacturing companies (mostly from the USA) set up factories with no real roots in the country. It often happened that when a left-wing government came to power many of these factories were closed. Between 1956 and 1968 alone, over 160 000 people emigrated from Jamaica to seek work elsewhere.

We can see how Jamaica's experience of overdependence on trade with developed industrial countries left it poor and politically unstable. The phrase 'Banana Republic' was coined disrespectfully to describe the Caribbean and Central American countries which depend on the export of a few raw materials in a market over which they have little control.

Iran

Bordered by the USSR, Turkey, Iraq, Afghanistan and Pakistan, Iran is a huge country of 1.65 million square km with a population of 37 million. Compare these figures with the countries in table 1.1. The capital, Tehran, has 4.5 million people. The GNP per capita is over $2000 per annum. From 1941 to 1979 Iran was ruled by the Shah, Mohammed Reza Pahlavi.

The key to the recent history of this mostly desert country lies in the oil deposits in the south-west, worked by the Anglo-Iranian oil company until nationalisation in 1951. A continuing struggle between Iran and the oil companies led to an agreement in 1973, followed immediately by the formation of OPEC (see page 81). This broke the power of the oil companies and promptly quadrupled the price of oil. The resulting bonanza financed the Shah's ambitious development schemes. But (a familiar picture) there was a lack of infrastructure, technical skill and expertise, which could not be provided even with expensive labour imported from developed countries.

Unexpectedly, and unfortunately for Iran, the price rises caused a marked drop in world demand for oil. Iran's income fell at a time when orders had been placed for new equipment. On top of these economic ills, there was growing religious opposition to the 'western style' of life which was being imported alongside other forms of modernisation. It was seen as decadent and as a threat to traditional religious values. In this situation the Shah's government adopted repressive measures to keep control of law and order. More

Part of the large oilfield in the mountains of south-west Iran

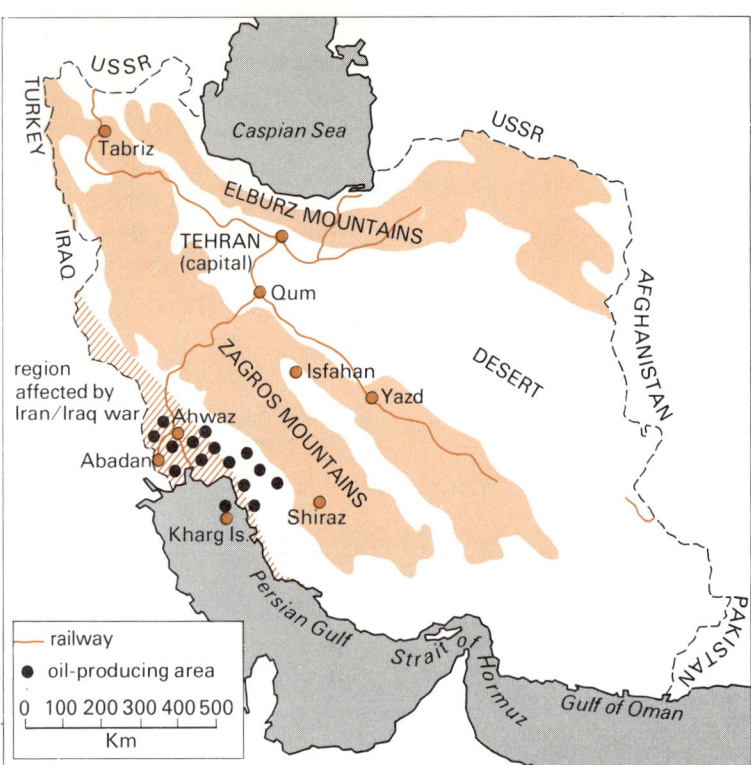

figure 9.3 Iran

than 60 000 people died in the period 1977-79 during a revolution which eventually overthrew the Shah and installed the religious leader Ayatollah Khomeni. By the start of the 1980s the production of oil had fallen sharply and rural life had suffered from a succession of development plans and political revolutions.

During this same period Iran experienced two disastrous earthquakes in addition to the drought and winter cold which are the permanent lot of most of Iran's rural population. The plight of this population was described in reports from international relief organisations. The rural communities were impoverished and disillusioned.

Most of the foreign 'advisers' departed, the Iran-Iraq war destroyed many oil pipelines and refineries and some minority population groups were demanding separation from Iran. Once more we can see how a country's development can suffer from overdependence on one commodity. And once again the attempt to transplant a western style of economy into an established, traditional society brought unrest and political instability. It seems that nations may attempt to 'develop' too rapidly when they think of development in Rostow terms (see fig. 7.5).

China

Contemplate the size of China before making any generalisations. This is the largest nation in the world and deserves careful study.

Mainland China's Nationalist Government was replaced in 1949 during Mao Tse Tung's Communist Revolution. At first China allied itself with the USSR but soon Mao produced his own style of communism. Mao charted a 'socialist road' to **collective** agriculture at village level, using huge production teams. In the first **five-year plan** (1953–57) the emphasis was on immediate creation of heavy industries, like steel, in huge capital-intensive complexes.

In 1958 a policy of 'walking on two legs' was announced, combining *technology-based, capital-intensive industries* with many *small-scale labour-intensive activities*. This produced 'The Great Leap Forward' which might be compared to Rostow's 'take-off' stage. But the 'leap' stumbled because of the lack of transport infrastructure and the low food output. This caused a further change in policy which gave priority to railways, tractors and fertiliser output.

The speed of the changes resulted in a period of self-criticism, the 'Cultural Revolution'. This checked the expansion of the bureaucracy and made it compulsory for all students, soldiers and intellectuals to work on the land for two years or more. During these years China became isolated from and mistrustful of 'the west', while its relations with the USSR deteriorated. Much economic momentum was lost.

When Mao died there were increased purges by a group called the 'Gang of Four'. They were overthrown by a new regime under Chairman Hua, who set about a dramatic attempt to heal the wounds of the cultural revolution. Contact was restored with 'the west'. Trade, tourism and technological progress were suddenly encouraged.

This is a complex story but the development stages for China can be summarised as follows:

1. Soviet-style heavy industry, collectivisation of agriculture: *First five-year plan*.
2. The *Great Leap Forward*: rapid expansion on all fronts making maximum use of China's great resource: manpower.
3. As the great leap faltered, the creation of more *small industries* and *better infrastructure*. Emphasis on development at local community level.
4. The *Cultural Revolution* and 'Gang of Four' purges, resulting in uncertainty, damage and delay to economic growth.

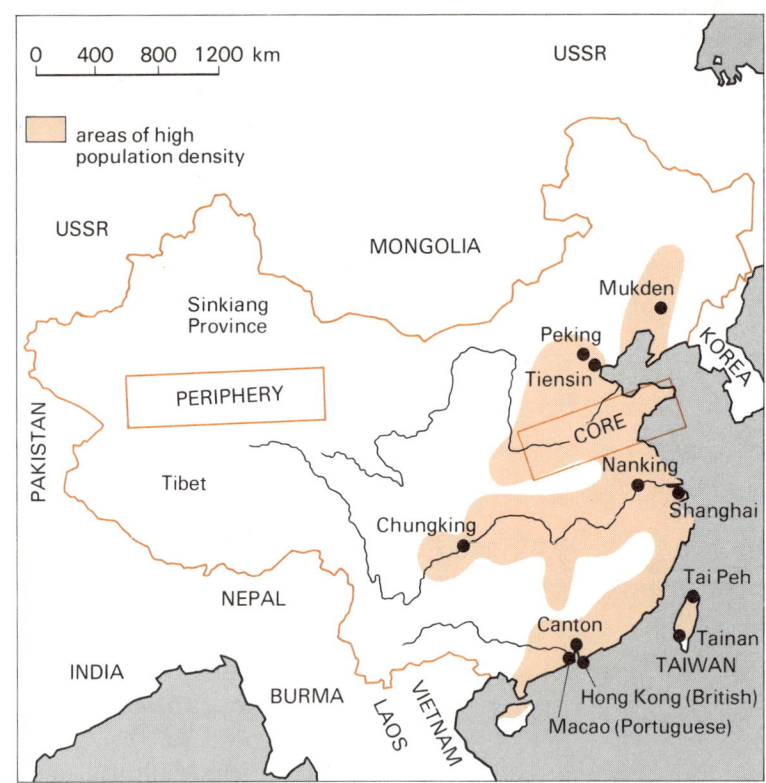

figure 9.4 China and Taiwan

力建设高度的社会主义物质文明和精神

What does this wall poster in Beijing (formerly called Peking) tell you about the Chinese perception of national development goals?

5. The drive to material prosperity and improved technology, including increased contact with the west, after 1977.

Taiwan

The defeated forces of the Nationalist Government of China took refuge in Taiwan (Formosa) in 1949. The island had been returned to China after the Japanese occupation in World War II. For strategic reasons the Japanese had built roads, airports and bridges and had also increased the island's agricultural output during the occupation. The exiled Nationalists gave land to the tenants and to millions of refugees from the mainland. The USA boosted the economy of the island because it saw Formosa as a buffer against communist China. Industry was developed so rapidly that GNP per capita reached $1100 in 1980. You will see many of the island's electronic goods, textiles and footwear on sale in the shops, often at prices lower than similar British products.

Taiwan's recent development history can be summarised as follows:

1. Infrastructure built by Japanese during World War II occupation. (During these years mainland China was ravaged by war.)
2. Land reform boosted farm output.
3. Light industry reduced dependence on imports.
4. Limited heavy industrial development.
5. Success of small textile and electronics firms.

It is just possible that during the 1980s China and Taiwan will become one country again. After rumours of plans to invade Taiwan from China and vice versa, there may now be a reconciliation. If that happens, which model of development will be adopted? Or will the two countries have evolved toward a common development model in the meantime?

Brazil

Brazil covers half of South America. (See fig. 6.6.) It illustrates the extremes of poverty and wealth which we have called **dualism** (page 62). Copacabana beach is the playground of the international millionaires while at the same time the squalid suburban *barradas* of the cities lack even the most basic amenities and services. The coastal cities continue to grow at alarming rates but the interior stagnates whilst its wealth is drawn towards the coastal cities. The Amazon Basin and the plateau are impoverished by 'backwash' (see fig. 7.6). Our map shows:

A. The interior *selvas* (equatorial forest) of the Amazon Basin and the *campos* (savannas) of the Brazilian Plateau. This is the economic *periphery* characterised by subsistence farming and extractive industries. Some of the

The Trans Amazonian Highway in Brazil

Why should so much money be invested in a motorway to cross such difficult terrain?

State	per 100 people		
	cars	telephones	hospital beds
Guanabara	59	70	76
São Paulo	45	56	47
Piauí	1	2	12
Ceará	3	7	16

surviving pockets of traditional tribal life are under threat from developments in mining and timber extraction. Some environmentalists think that the destruction of the selvas could even damage the earth's atmosphere.

B. The farms and plantations worked by descendants of the Portuguese settlers and negro slaves. In the extreme south, the mixed farms established by settlers of German origin show a more balanced economy.

C. The economic **core** of Brazil on its eastern margin. The growth of São Paulo can be shown thus:

Year	1936	1950	1958	1963	1967	1971	1975
Population (millions)	1	2	3	4	5	6	7

The heavy industry (steel, automobiles) and the light industry (e.g. electronics) and the high technology (e.g. aircraft) are all concentrated in this coastal zone. Many of them draw upon the minerals, labour and other resources of the interior.

figure 9.5 Brazil

Summary

In this chapter we have considered how some of the theory covered earlier in the book helps to explain patterns of development in:

- Ghana — industrialisation on a weak base
- Jamaica — problems caused by overdependence on trade with developed countries
- Iran — rapid industrialisation strained the economy and traditions of the population
- China — an example of centrally planned development
- Taiwan — rapid industrialisation, encouraged by political factors
- Brazil — marked contrasts in development between the core and periphery (dualism)

Exercises

1 Use the information in this chapter and your atlas and reference books to:
(a) draw a diagram like fig. 8.3 illustrating 'The pattern of development in Brazil'.
(b) compare it with models earlier in this book.

2 Choose a country other than the ones featured in this chapter. Draw a simple sketch map of the country chosen.
Draw a table to show how the 'reasons for differences in development' explored in chapter 8 relate to the chosen country.
Construct a diagram to illustrate the country's level of technology and transport network (see fig. 7.5).

3 Draw a simplified map of the northern hemisphere with the North Pole at the centre (you will find such a polar projection in an atlas). It will show the relative positions of USA, USSR and China. From information in an atlas, show the distribution of the three giants' major resources: coal, oil and cereal land. Locate the major centres of industry and population. If you can find the information (it is shown in the Pan *State of the World Atlas*), also show the positions of missiles and 'defence' lines.
   Comment on the pattern which emerges.

4 Using the map and statistics in fig. 9.5,
(a) draw maps to represent the statistics;
(b) draw graphs (see fig. 6.4) to represent the statistics;
(c) summarise what they tell you about patterns of well-being and development in Brazil;
(d) comment on the value of these statistics as measures of well-being and indicators of development styles;
(e) compare any of these statistics with the equivalent for your school or class.

10 Develop your own country

This chapter gives you the opportunity to plan the growth of an imaginary third world country, 'Barota', located just north of the equator. You will have the opportunity to tackle the kinds of problems people and governments throughout the world have had to face. Can you do any better than they have done? You have the advantage of being able to look back at their experiences and to use some of the ideas you have read about in the earlier chapters of this book.

The Republic of Barota

Barota is a developing country situated between the Equator and the Tropic of Cancer. It is 750 km from east to west and 600 km from north to south. You will not find it in any atlas, because it is purely fictional. Despite this, it is a realistic model incorporating many of the environmental, social, political and economic problems common to many tropical 'third world' countries in Africa and South America. Your task is to understand some of these problems and then to decide on the greatest priorities upon which to spend limited financial resources in order to improve the economy of this poor country.

You have been provided with the following resources:

1. Relief map of Barota (fig. 10.1). Copies of this outline map can also be used to locate possible development projects, new roads, etc.

2. Block diagram to show the physical environment of Barota (fig. 10.2).

3. Two transects drawn from fig. 10.2 (fig. 10.3).

4. Economic map of Barota (fig. 10.4).

5. Details of population structure and distribution (fig. 10.5).

6. Table showing possible development projects (table 10.1). (See page 97.)

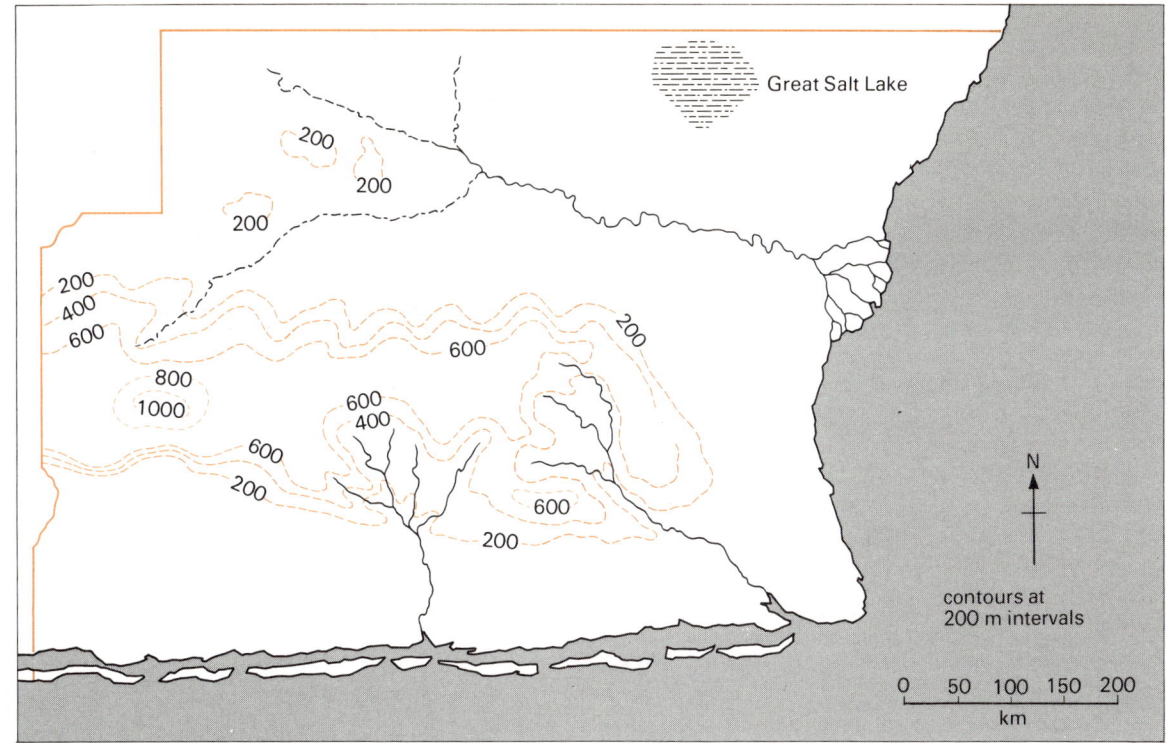

figure 10.1 'Barota': physical

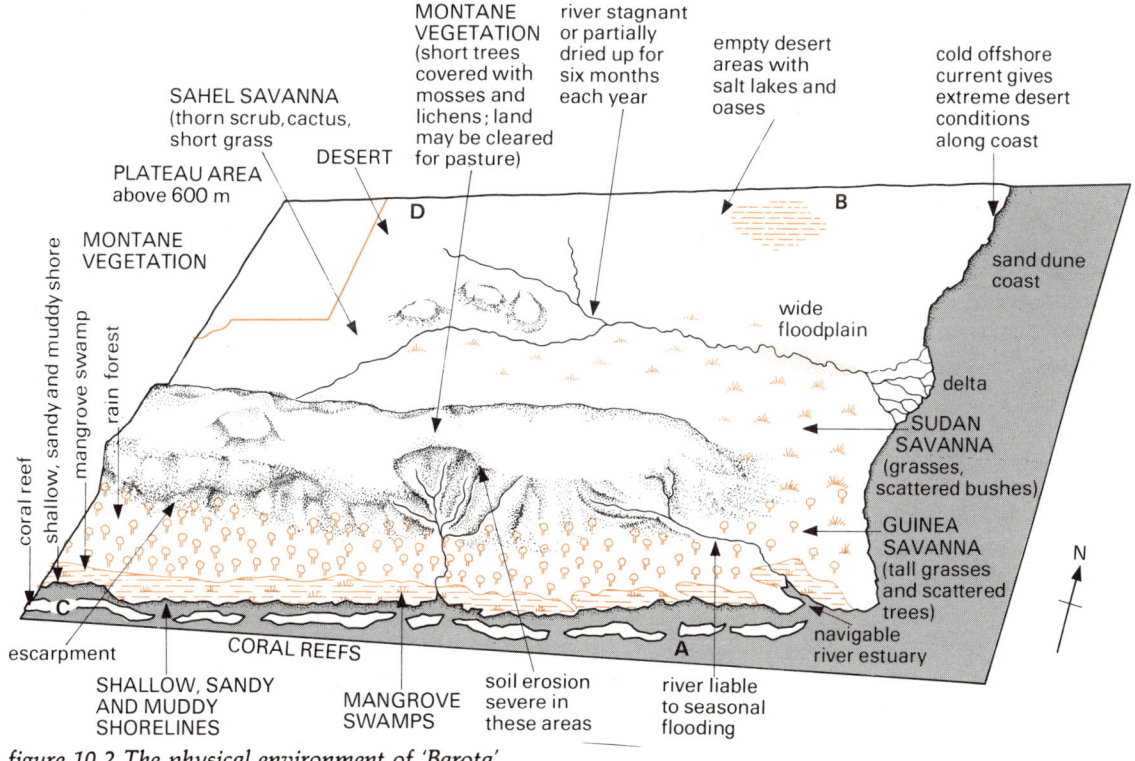

figure 10.2 The physical environment of 'Barota'

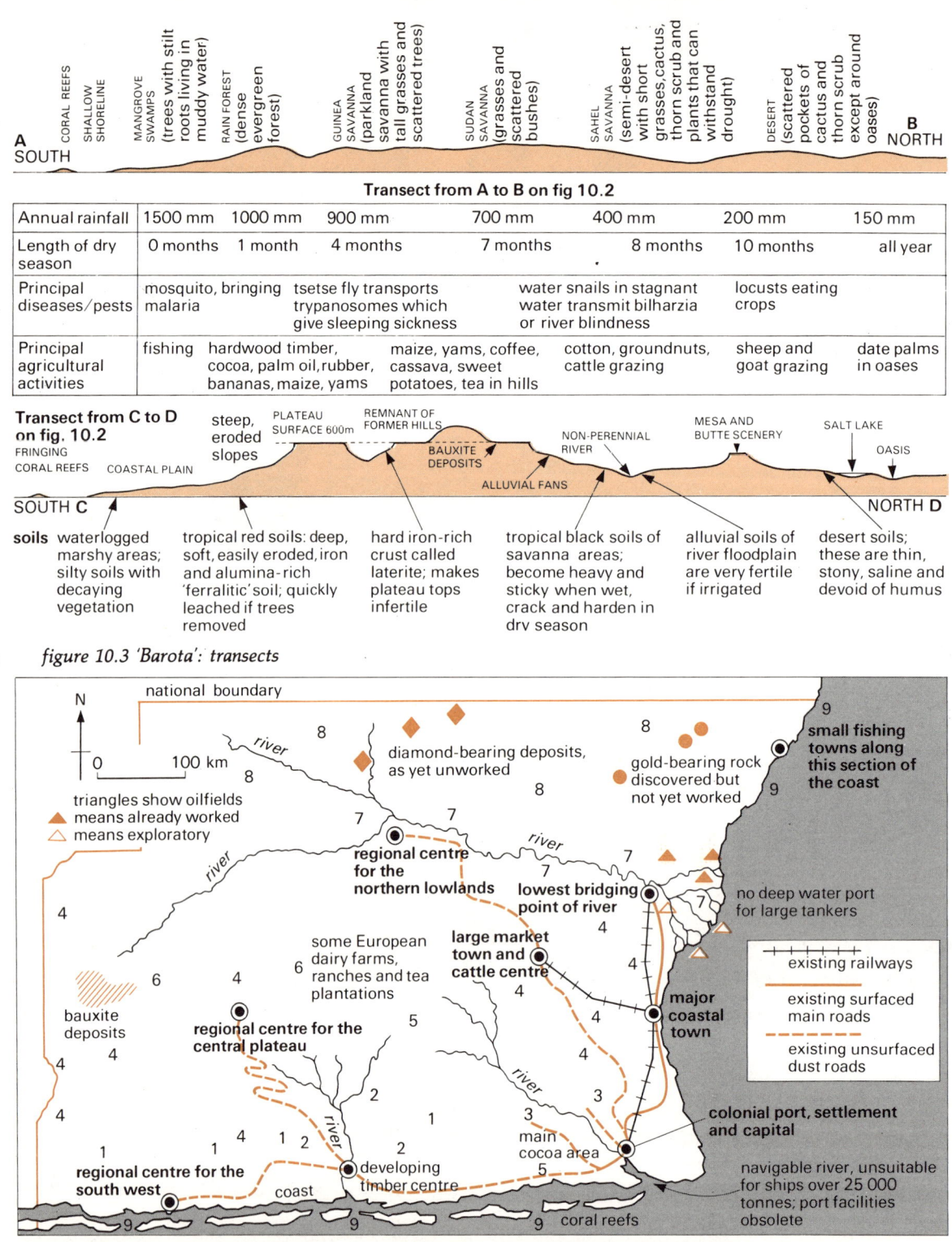

Transect from A to B on fig 10.2

Labels (SOUTH → NORTH): CORAL REEFS · SHALLOW SHORELINE · MANGROVE SWAMPS (trees with stilt roots living in muddy water) · RAIN FOREST (dense evergreen forest) · GUINEA SAVANNA (parkland savanna with tall grasses and scattered trees) · SUDAN SAVANNA (grasses and scattered bushes) · SAHEL SAVANNA (semi-desert with short grasses, cactus, thorn scrub and plants that can withstand drought) · DESERT (scattered pockets of cactus and thorn scrub except around oases)

A SOUTH — B NORTH

Annual rainfall	1500 mm	1000 mm	900 mm	700 mm	400 mm	200 mm	150 mm
Length of dry season	0 months	1 month	4 months	7 months	8 months	10 months	all year
Principal diseases/pests	mosquito, bringing malaria	tsetse fly transports trypanosomes which give sleeping sickness		water snails in stagnant water transmit bilharzia or river blindness		locusts eating crops	
Principal agricultural activities	fishing	hardwood timber, cocoa, palm oil, rubber, bananas, maize, yams		maize, yams, coffee, cassava, sweet potatoes, tea in hills	cotton, groundnuts, cattle grazing	sheep and goat grazing	date palms in oases

Transect from C to D on fig. 10.2

Labels: FRINGING CORAL REEFS · COASTAL PLAIN · steep, eroded slopes · PLATEAU SURFACE 600m · REMNANT OF FORMER HILLS · BAUXITE DEPOSITS · ALLUVIAL FANS · NON-PERENNIAL RIVER · MESA AND BUTTE SCENERY · SALT LAKE · OASIS

SOUTH C — NORTH D

soils	waterlogged marshy areas; silty soils with decaying vegetation	tropical red soils: deep, soft, easily eroded, iron and alumina-rich 'ferralitic' soil; quickly leached if trees removed	hard iron-rich crust called laterite; makes plateau tops infertile	tropical black soils of savanna areas; become heavy and sticky when wet, crack and harden in dry season	alluvial soils of river floodplain are very fertile if irrigated	desert soils; these are thin, stony, saline and devoid of humus

figure 10.3 'Barota': transects

Map labels (figure 10.4): national boundary · N · 0 — 100 km · triangles show oilfields ▲ means already worked △ means exploratory · diamond-bearing deposits, as yet unworked · gold-bearing rock discovered but not yet worked · small fishing towns along this section of the coast · regional centre for the northern lowlands · lowest bridging point of river · no deep water port for large tankers · some European dairy farms, ranches and tea plantations · large market town and cattle centre · bauxite deposits · regional centre for the central plateau · major coastal town · existing railways · existing surfaced main roads · existing unsurfaced dust roads · main cocoa area · colonial port, settlement and capital · regional centre for the south west · developing timber centre · coast · coral reefs · navigable river, unsuitable for ships over 25 000 tonnes; port facilities obsolete

1 shifting agriculture 3 cooperative farming 5 plantations 7 irrigated farming 9 fishing
2 forestry 4 subsistence cropping 6 European farms 8 pastoral

figure 10.4 'Barota': economic

96

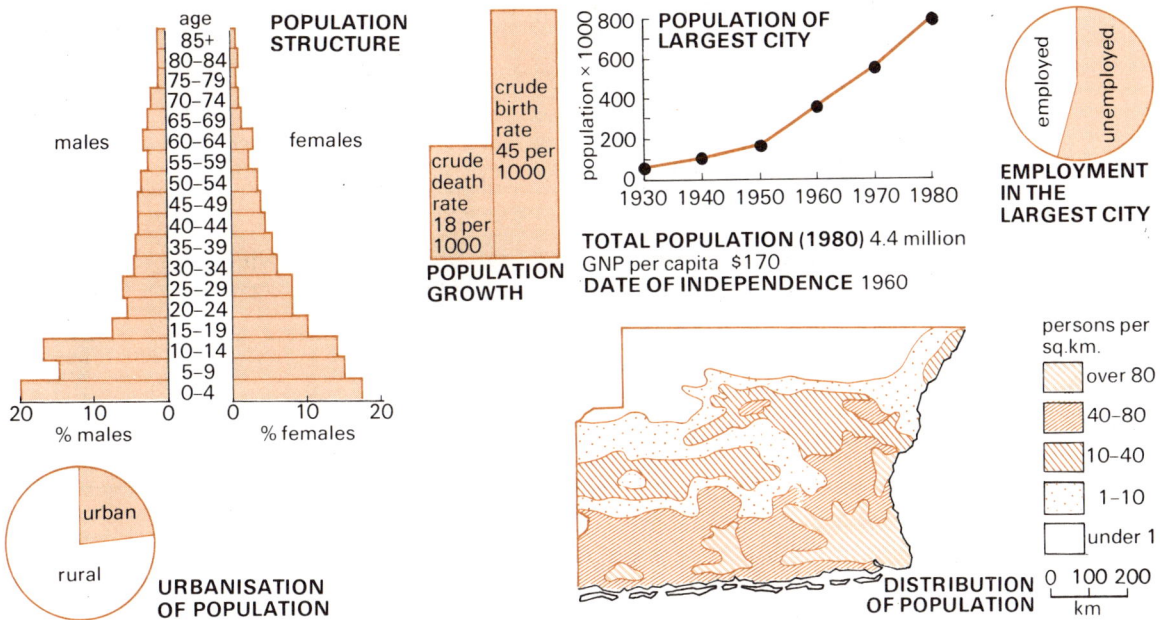

figure 10.5 Population statistics for 'Barota'

table 10.1   Possible development projects for the Republic of Barota

Scheme letter	Proposed scheme	Unit cost
A	Construction of a new capital city to administer the new republic. Well planned buildings and gardens would replace the colonial structures.	1
B	Dam and reservoir to supply water for a major irrigation project.	1
C	National game park. A protected area to preserve wildlife and develop tourism.	1
D	Purchasing of 500 tractors from Europe to be distributed to farmers throughout Barota.	½
E	The establishment of an effective and free family planning service.	½
F	The development of a bauxite mine, including the purchase of a dragline, earth moving equipment and a crushing plant (but not a rail or road link from outside).	½
G	The construction of a large teaching hospital which will have a special research section specialising in tropical diseases.	½
H	Money to finance further oil exploration work in the delta region.	1
I	The construction of a large automated textile mill to process cotton grown in Barota.	½
J	The construction of five large tourist hotels furnished to international standards. Three will be on the coast and two in the game park.	½
K	The establishment of free primary education for all children between 6 and 11.	1

Scheme letter	Proposed scheme	Unit cost
L	The establishment of Air Barota with three ex Pan-Am Boeing 747 'jumbo jets' and the construction of an International Airport with a runway suitable for these aircraft and with modern air traffic control facilities.	1
M	The building of a brewery and a beer bottling/canning factory.	½
N	A new deepwater port to replace the obsolete port at present serving Barota. This port could handle bulk carriers, container ships and cruise liners.	1
O	The construction of a dam, reservoir and a hydro-electric power station to generate cheap electricity without importing fuel.	½
P	The construction of an integrated iron and steel works using imported raw materials.	1
Q	The establishment of the University of Barota, initially just with the faculties of Arts and Science.	½
R	Soil conservation scheme to control and reclaim land damaged or destroyed by soil erosion, including re-afforestation and terracing.	½
S	The construction of fifty simple rural medical centres with clinics and dispensaries staffed by medical orderlies. These centres could deal with simple health problems (e.g. child care, injections, broken limbs, dietary complaints etc.) but not with complex medical cases (e.g. heart or brain surgery, cancer etc).	½
T	The establishment of ten rural agricultural development centres which would develop improved varieties of seeds, and would train local farmers to increase crop yields by using more efficient farming methods.	½
U	A cigarette factory and tobacco growing scheme to reduce the amount of money being spent on importing cigarettes from Europe and the USA.	½
V	Improving Barota's road network by either 300 km of unsurfaced roads, or 150 km of surfaced roads, or any combination of the two not exceeding the total value of either option. Note that unsurfaced roads may be impassable during parts of the rainy season. Barota's present road network is shown on fig. 10.4.	1
W	Extending the rail network by 100 km, including the purchasing of diesel locomotives and passenger and freight rolling stock for this new extension. The present rail network is shown on fig. 10.4.	1
X	At present the country has no means of defence against foreign invasion or insurgency from rebels within. There have been threats from the northern state, and there are deep divisions between the nomadic tribesmen of the north and the farmers of the south. An armed police force/security guard, ten helicopters, a squadron of ground attack/trainer aircraft and three coastal patrol boats are required by the Chief of the Barotan Armed Force.	1
Y	You may use ½ or 1 unit to extend or repeat a unit already chosen (e.g. 600 km of unsurfaced roads, 150 km of railway etc.) provided that you do not exceed the 6 unit maximum allowed.	

The background

Under the headings *relief, climate, soils, agriculture, distribution of population*, write a descriptive report of the geography of Barota, using the resources provided.

Strategies for development

Explain why it is essential for Barota to develop the following things. (Write a paragraph on each.)

    agricultural improvements
    a larger road and rail network
    power supplies
    water control
    better health facilities
    an educational system

Allocating resources

A limited amount of capital to be spent over the next five years is available from oil revenues, exports of cocoa, cotton, palm oil etc., tourism, aid, and loans from the World Bank to finance *six full units* of value from table 10.1. You must decide how you are going to spend these six units by making the combination that you feel is most appropriate, from either half or whole units.

Having decided on your six units, you must then thoroughly justify your choice. Any recommendations that you make should be clearly recorded on a copy of fig. 10.1 or on a map of your own design.

Obviously the best combinations will be those that help to solve the most acute problems of the country, and which are well integrated with each other. None of the major problems of this country can be solved in five years, so you should indicate how the next allocation of money might be spent to continue the projects that you have commenced. You should consider the balance that you strike between large capital projects and small community schemes, and the balance between social and wealth-creating improvements.

11 Towards the 21st century

It is estimated that by the year 2000 some three quarters of the world's population will be in those countries which we called 'less developed'.

Will food supply increase?
Will population growth continue?
Will energy supplies last?
Will there be political stability?
Will the quality of life improve?

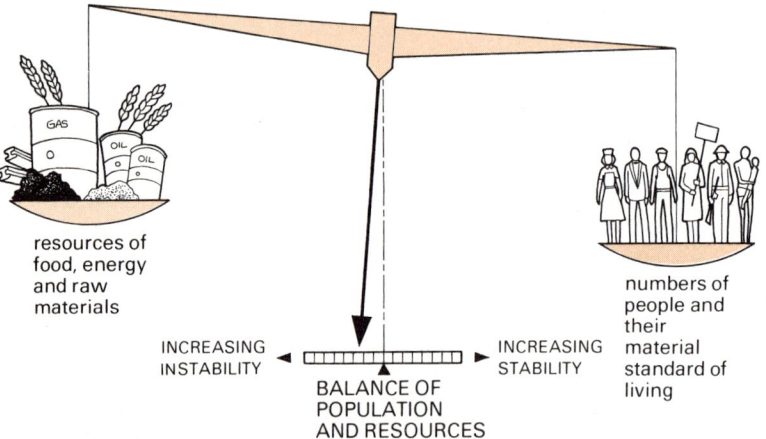

figure 11.1 The balance of population and resources

If the number of people and their standard of living place too big a load on available resources, the result will be instability in the political, economic, social and ecological systems. This will increase the likelihood of war, famine, unrest, pollution and environmental deterioration unless levels of technology can advance.

The 1970s started with a feeling that the third world problems could be solved by a combination of population policy and economic progress through capital investment and new technology. This showed a degree of confidence in the 'Rostow' model (see fig. 7.5). But things did not always work out as planned: some of the new chemicals, drugs and 'miracle seeds' were less than successful. They often had unexpected side-effects. They were usually unavailable to those in greatest need. Furthermore, the 1973 OPEC price rises (page 87) had an unpredicted serious effect on the world economy, on trade and on money supplies. It was obvious at the start of the 1980s that there were no simple solutions. Predictions concerning development proved as unreliable as the population predictions we looked at earlier.

There is a very complex relationship between these variables which affect future world prosperity:

    population size
    food supply
    level of technology
    resource reserves
    pollution
    standard of living

Many attempts are made to predict the consequences of some of the more likely trends. One such prediction is summarised in fig. 11.2. It is the work of the Massachusetts Institute of Technology. According to these predictions it seems certain that:

1. Unrestricted population growth will result in the sort of disastrous 'controls' envisaged by Malthus (page 30): disease, famine and wars.

2. If we attempt to provide even the most basic living standards for an increasing population the result will be (a) rapid exhaustion of resources, (b) pollution of the air, soil and water to critical levels.

3. The only way to avoid environmental disaster and to ensure stability is to (a) contain population growth *and* (b) restrict the consumption of natural resources, thus (c) avoiding resource exhaustion and critical pollution.

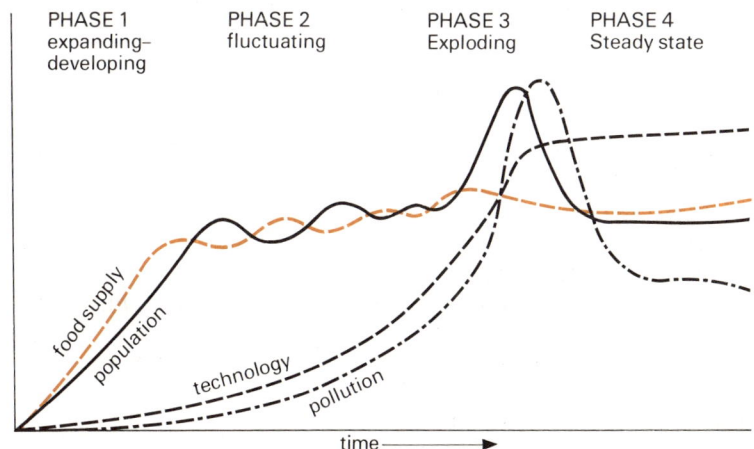

figure 11.2 Predictive trends for development

Summary

The main aim of this book has been to introduce you to a number of key ideas about population and economic development. These ideas have involved learning a range of skills and techniques of analysis which you should find useful even after completing your examination course. More importantly, however, we hope you are now aware of your own values and attitudes towards other countries and cultures. In the last chapter we have explored these ideas:

- There are no simple solutions to development problems and a lot of variable factors affect future development patterns
- These variables are difficult to assess but it is possible to predict the consequences of unrestrained growth of population, appetites and technology
- Unrestrained growth would affect
  raw material and fuel reserves
  standards of well-being
  migration
  political stability
  social stability
- The control of appetites, technology, pollution, population and resources, all involve questions of religion, morality, ethics and politics
- It is impossible to discuss these vital questions without a background of factual information, a knowledge of processes, the use of skills and ideas such as those presented in this book, together with a flexibility of attitudes

Exercises

1 Table 11.1 is offered purely as a stimulus for thought and discussion. Read it through, contemplate and discuss it.
(a) List any evidence you can find that these predictions are coming true.
(b) How fast are the predictions likely to come true?
(c) Which of them are already demonstrably inaccurate?
(d) Make your own list of predictions and suggest some possible courses of action.

2 Copy fig. 11.2 as far as phase 3 and then show what would happen after:
(a) continued population growth,
(b) continued population growth accompanied by unchanged food output,
(c) continued population growth accompanied by increased food output,
(d) continued technical advance.

table 11.1   Thinking about the future

Theme	Possible future trends	Possible outcomes/solutions
Rapid population growth	World population may double in 40 years	A world population of 8000 million by 2010?
Rapid urban growth, especially in third world	Major increase in unplanned spontaneous settlements	Nearly 60% of world's population will be urbanised by 2000 (about 40% in 1980)
Increase in number of retired people; increased life expectancy	Number of over-sixty-year-olds may rise by nearly 100% between 1980 and 2000	Increased strain on hospitals, housing, food, doctors, etc.
Natural disasters, such as volcanic eruptions, landslides, earthquakes	More areas will be reclaimed and settled, and, with the world population nearly doubled, there will be more people at risk	There will be more fatalities and people made homeless. Disaster relief agencies will need to become better organised.
Wildlife and landscape conservation; control of pollution	Environmental groups will demand increasingly tight controls on industrial and mining activities	There will be an increase in costs of raw material and finished products
Health and disease	Drugs, pesticides and improved sanitation will continue to improve people's health	The poorest people in the world will probably still be beyond the reach of the benefits of modern medicine
Land reform in rural areas	Much land will probably be unfairly distributed in 2000, but the position will be better than in 1980	World food output will still be hindered by inefficient and unjust land holding. Will food be better distributed?
'Green revolution' raising food yields	Despite setbacks caused by disease and wrong applications, progress will be be made	At best, food supply will keep up with population growth
Increased energy needs	Oil and coal reserves may be considerably depleted	Alternative sources of energy and more energy-efficient industrial processes and transport will be invented. Energy prices may soar beyond the reach of very poor countries
Increased third world industrialisation	Industries processing tropical commodities and labour-intensive industries will be developed rapidly in the third world, at the expense of the western world	Competition from developing countries in the world market place for low/medium technology products will cause unemployment in the developed world

Theme	Possible future trends	Possible outcomes/solutions
Increased mechanisation in industry	Computers and robots will become increasingly important in data processing and assembly work	Mechanisation will affect high technology countries more than third world countries, who cannot afford the cost
Development of *intermediate*, or *appropriate*, technology	Increasingly the third world countries will develop their own type of technology	Improved agriculture, less drudgery and many more small village industries will help the third world greatly
Infrastructure improvements	There will be a great increase in road, rail, power station, reservoir, seaport and airport construction	Increased accessibility will assist rural areas and help prevent dualism. Poor peoples sometimes will suffer from isolation
Technological dependence of the third world on the developed world	Despite intermediate technology, the third world will continue to require technical help, especially with transport, industrial machinery and defence equipment	There will be a higher level of technical breakdowns and accidents in the third world. Obsolete equipment may be poorly maintained or inappropriately used
Education and adult literacy	Some people will be inappropriately trained, and many will continue to lack sufficient education	Education and retraining will still be inadequate. In some countries, literacy rates will fall
Revival of religious and ethnic awareness	Militant Islamic culture, Buddhism, Evangelical Christianity, Roman Catholicism and regional cultures will probably all assert themselves more fully. Separatist movements will increase in number	The standardised pattern of western development will be modified, slowed or rejected by a number of nations anxious to develop their cultural identities
Wars, revolutions, internal unrest, law and order	There are many sources of tension and injustice. There is no evidence to suggest that the level of violence will decline in the next 20 years; it might well increase	Putting aside the impossible and unthinkable question of nuclear warfare, urban violence and terrorist activity is likely to increase continuously
The role of women in society	In many third world countries, women do much of the food growing; they provide very cheap labour and have few rights	Whilst there will certainly be a trend towards increased personal freedom for women, many third world women will remain underprivileged

Theme	Possible future trends	Possible outcomes/solutions
Racial discrimination	In many multiracial societies there is discrimination	Racial tensions are likely to continue, perhaps causing serious civil unrest
Imposed cultural standards	Through trade, ex-colonial links, media, advertising, tourism or aid, values of a developed country may be imposed on a developing country	Imposed cultural standards may raise expectations unduly, or may damage the fabric of society
Aid to developing countries	The need to increase aid is certainly there, but not the will. This may continue to be the case	Aid money may well be levied on developed countries and not just 'donated'
Trade controls and price agreements	It is possible that other commodity groups will follow the OPEC pattern and form protective price **cartels**	Costs of raw materials to the developed world will increase, giving increased inflation
Multinational company policies	Multinational companies may well increase their hold of world trade still further	More economic decisions may be placed in the hands of big business rather than in governments or communities
Tourism	Tourism has continually increased amongst richer peoples	Tourism will probably increase, but at a slower rate
Which economic model to choose?	The choices range from centralised growth poles to regional dispersion	There will probably be an increasing trend towards regionally dispersed development

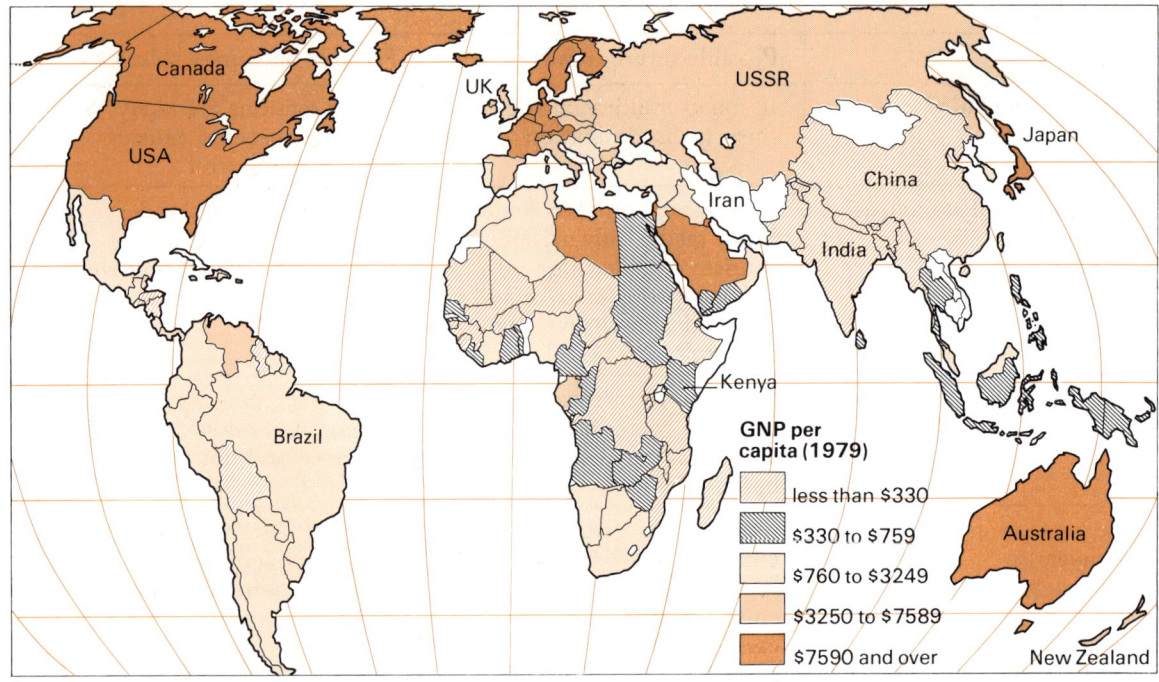

figure 11.3 World population and GNP per capita (from the **World Bank Atlas**, 1981)

Populations of 1 million or more, ranked by number of population

	Population (thousands)		Population (thousands)		Population (thousands)
China	981 812	Morocco	19 538	Cameroon	8245
India	659 590	Algeria	18 260	Ivory Coast	8227
USSR	264 115	Sudan	17 862	Ecuador	8081
United States	223 631	Taiwan	17 800	Austria	7491
Indonesia	142 870	Tanzania	17 538	Zimbabwe	7146
Brazil	116 539	Korea, Democratic		Angola	6901
Japan	115 692	People's Republic of	17 474	Guatemala	6811
Bangladesh	87 668	Peru	17 149	Mali	6750
Nigeria	82 603			Switzerland	6458
Pakistan	79 705	German Democratic		Tunisia	6194
		Republic	16 846		
Mexico	65 509	Afghanistan	15 542	Kampuchea	6000
Germany, Federal		Kenya	15 274	Malawi	5817
Republic of	61 159	Czechoslovakia	15 236	Yemen Arab Republic	5718
Italy	56 764	Sri Lanka	14 542	Upper Volta	5642
United Kingdom	55 940			Zambia	5580
France	53 380	Venezuela	14 453		
		Australia	14 321	Senegal	5518
Vietnam	52 943	Netherlands, The	14 007	Bolivia	5428
Philippines	46 748	Nepal	13 963	Dominican Republic	5280
Thailand	45 475	Malaysia	13 137	Guinea	5275
Turkey	44 237			Niger	5163
Egypt, Arab		Uganda	12 797		
Republic of	38 868	Iraq	12 631	Denmark	5112
		Ghana	11 313	Hong Kong	4965
Korea, Republic of	37 814	Chile	10 917	Rwanda	4947
Spain	37 033	Hungary	10 716	Haiti	4921
Iran	36 971			Finland	4835
Poland	35 436	Mozambique	10 199		
Burma	32 573	Belgium	9829	El Salvador	4410
		Portugal	9771	Chad	4365
Ethiopia	30 861	Cuba	9760	Norway	4066
South Africa	28 469	Greece	9272	Burundi	4022
Zaire	27 509			Somalia	3828
Argentina	27 313	Bulgaria	8951		
Colombia	26 122	Syrian Arab Republic	8639	Israel	3783
		Saudi Arabia	8606	Honduras	3563
Canada	23 690	Madagascar	8480	Puerto Rico	3547
Yugoslavia	22 139	Sweden	8264	Benin	3425
Romania	22 068			Sierra Leone	3381

	Population (thousands)		Population (thousands)		Population (thousands)
Lao People's Democratic Republic	3349	Nicaragua	2584	Mauritania	1588
Ireland	3272	Togo	2420	Congo, People's Republic of the	1497
New Zealand	3234	Singapore	2361	Lesotho	1309
Jordan	3126	Central African Republic	2245	Kuwait	1279
Paraguay	2974	Costa Rica	2162	Bhutan	1267
Papua New Guinea	2939	Jamaica	2159	Trinidad and Tobago	1150
Uruguay	2904	Yemen, People's Democratic Republic of	1855		
Libya	2862	Liberia	1797		
Albania	2670	Panama	1794		
Lebanon	2662	Mongolia	1622		

Populations of 1 million or more, ranked by amount of per capita GNP. GNP per capita rounded to nearest US $10.

	GNP per capita Amount 1979 (US $)		GNP per capita Amount 1979 (US $)		GNP per capita Amount 1979 (US $)
Kuwait	20 250	Brazil	1770	Yemen, People's Democratic Republic of	370
Switzerland	15 360	Costa Rica	1630	Madagascar	330
Sweden	12 250	Panama	1550	Mauritania	300
Germany, Federal Republic of	12 200	Korea, Republic of	1510	Niger	300
Denmark	12 030	Malaysia	1450	Uganda	290
Norway	11 230	Turkey	1380	Central African Republic	280
Belgium	11 020	Jordan	1200	Benin	270
France	10 650	Syrian Arab Republic	1170	Guinea	270
United States	10 610	Tunisia	1160	Pakistan	270
Netherlands, The	10 490	Paraguay	1140	China	260
Saudi Arabia	9960	Ecuador	1110	Mozambique	250
Canada	9410	Jamaica	1110	Sierra Leone	250
Austria	9130	Ivory Coast	1070	Tanzania	250
Australia	8870	Colombia	1060	Afghanistan	240
Japan	8730	Dominican Republic	1030	Haiti	230
Finland	8520	Guatemala	1010	Sri Lanka	230
Libya	8480	Mongolia	940	Malawi	220
United Kingdom	7390	Nigeria	910	India	210
New Zealand	6400	Peru	850	Zaire	210
German Democratic Republic	6310	Cuba	810	Burundi	190
Italy	5730	Morocco	780	Rwanda	190
Czechoslovakia	5190	Papua New Guinea	760	Mali	180
Spain	4920	Albania	740	Upper Volta	180
Ireland	4480	N. Korea	730	Vietnam	170
Israel	4230	Congo, People's Republic of the	670	Burma	150
Greece	4140	El Salvador	640	Nepal	130
USSR	4040	Philippines	640	Somalia	130
Trinidad and Tobago	3910	Nicaragua	610	Chad	120
Hungary	3780	Thailand	600	Ethiopia	120
Poland	3770	Cameroon	590	Bangladesh	110
Singapore	3770	Bolivia	550	Laos	90
Hong Kong	3640	Zimbabwe	550	Bhutan	80
Bulgaria	3630	Zambia	540	Iran	n.a.
Venezuela	3440	Honduras	520	Kampuchea	n.a.
Puerto Rico	2840	Liberia	520	Lebanon	n.a.
Iraq	2710	Egypt, Arab Republic of	500		
Uruguay	2500	Senegal	450		
Yugoslavia	2370	Sudan	450		
Argentina	2210	Angola	430		
Romania	2100	Yemen Arab Republic	420		
Portugal	2060	Ghana	400		
South Africa	2000	Togo	400		
Chile	1890	Kenya	390		
Mexico	1880	Indonesia	370		
Algeria	1770	Lesotho	370		

Analysis of chapter content

	Terminology and ideas	Skills and techniques	Context
Chapter 1 **Population patterns**	population size population characteristics population density population distribution range and mode regular, random, cluster conurbation perception	estimating questioning opinion surveys interpreting data visualising evaluating hypothesis testing discussing **line graph** **isotype** **ranking** **bar graph** **pie chart** **mapping data**	home football crowd school home town Leeds London Edinburgh Britain North America all continents world

Chapter 2
What kinds of people live
where?
	anthropology
	Homo sapiens
	mammal, primate
	common, peculiar
	negroid, caucasoid,
	   mongoloid
	segregation
	adaptive radiation
	differentiation, variables
	census
	well-being
	mental models
	concentric model
		analysing
		correlating
		testing ideas
		matching map and photo
		detecting bias
		written explanation
		modifying models
		choropleth map
		transect
		analysing newspaper
		   adverts
			school
			city
			distant lands
			home town

Chapter 3
Population dynamics
	birth rate, death rate
	natural change
	volume, flow
	immigration, emigration
	net migration
	population explosion
	demography
	fertility
	population policy
	amenities
	cohort
	age/sex structure
	population pyramid
	demographic transition
		calculating population size
		graphing population
		   change
		analysing graphs
		analysing cartoons
		interpreting news reports
		predicting
		analysing attitudes
		constructing **population**
		   pyramids
		analysing **population**
		   pyramids
		drawing cartoons
			school
			neighbourhood
			Yorkshire
			Britain
			Germany
			third world
			world

Chapter 4 **People on the move**	journeys daily rhythms frequency, duration territory, migration push-pull migration models rural–urban migration infrastructure	classifying movement graphing movement mapping migration **migration models** **topological maps** **block diagram**	house town home region Portugal Alps world

	Terminology and ideas	Skills and techniques	Context

Chapter 5
Worlds apart
	location
	distance
	change
	native
	sedentary, nomadic
	transhumance
	nationality, race
	average income
	temperate latitudes
	conservative
	different lifestyles
	different values
		analysing secondhand
		  experiences
		synthesising experiences
		comparing and
		  contrasting
		using maps to show
		  location
		  distance
		  area
		  latitude
		interpreting **population**
		  pyramids
		evaluating **photos** and
		  cartoons
		questioning situations
			Kenya
			Japan

Chapter 6
Patterns of wealth and
poverty
	quality of life
	life expectancy
	National Mean Income
	Gross National Product
	Physical Quality of Life
	  Index
	First, Second, Third
	  World
	Brandt Report
	North–South
	aid
		plotting variables
		correlating variables
		devising prosperity indices
		graphs: correlation
			home
			home area
			Birmingham
			Nairobi

Chapter 7
Development in action
	shifting subsistence
	  agriculture
	dependence
	social stability
	appropriate technology
	less developed country
	Rostow model
	dualism, growth pole
	core–periphery
	prestige projects
	swash–backwash
	balanced economy
	capitalism, communism
	primary, secondary,
	  tertiary
		matching graphs and
		  pictures
		graphing
		mapping
		development models
		block diagrams
			farm
			region
			nations
			USA
			Botswana
			world

Chapter 8
Regional differences in
development
	upland
	tropical colony
	granite highland
	outflow
	tourism, commuter
	metropolitan core
	hinterland
	natural advantages
	inhospitable environments
	resource endowment
	world trade organisations
	technological
	  developments
	farming types
	green revolution
	nodal, remote
	superpowers
	imperialism
	communist satellites
	'wilderness'
	isolates
	stability
		mapping
		planning
		predicting
		detecting conflict
		models
		Venn diagram
		using the media to update
		  development models
			worldwide coverage on
			a regional and national
			scale

	Ideas	Context
Chapter 9 **Examples of development** **in practice**	This chapter illustrates and applies the preceding ideas and skills in a selection of countries.	Ghana Jamaica Iran China Taiwan Brazil
Chapter 10 **Develop your own** **country**	This chapter is a simulation involving the practice and application of the skills and ideas presented in preceding chapters. Given certain information, students have to plan the development of a fictitious third world country, Barota.	
Chapter 11 **Towards the 21st** **century**	A concluding chapter which briefly considers the various inter-related factors which will influence future World development and population growth.	

Glossary

adaptive radiation A process whereby a species spreads outwards into new territory and adapts to changing conditions.

annual Every year.

anthropology The study of man as an animal.

apartheid In South Africa, the policy of separate development of racial groups.

appropriate technology Simple machinery, easy and cheap to operate and maintain, may be more appropriate to a non-technical community in a developing region.

backwash A counterwave returning against the main flow (see *swash*).

basic literacy The ability to read and write.

bridge point A convenient point to build a bridge over a river.

cartel A manufacturer's union to control production, marketing and prices.

caucasoid One of the three main groups of people distinguished by anthropologists: the fair-skinned people originating in Europe, West Asia and the Middle East.

CBD The Central Business District of a town, where the main shops and offices are concentrated.

census A population count.

centrally planned economy When a government controls the key parts of a nation's economy.

choropleth map A map shaded or coloured in blocks to show areas falling between two given values (e.g. between 20 and 40 people per square kilometre).

collective farming Where farms group together under common ownership to share labour, equipment, land and buildings, working together to sell the produce and share the profits.

cohort see *population cohort*.

conurbation The growth of towns to the stage where they join with neighbouring towns to form one large urbanised mass or conurbation.

core A centre of growth.

core commodities Important key materials for industrial processing.

correlation A comparison between two variable quantities seeking to establish a relationship between them.

crude birth rate The ratio of the number of people born to the number of people in an area during a given period.

crude death rate The ratio of the number of people who died to the number of people living in an area in a given period.

demography The study of population.

development aid Funds provided to assist economic growth, especially in needy areas.

dispersion diagram A graph showing the spread of a collection of numbers.

distribution – clustered grouped together
        random haphazard or irregular
        regular evenly spread.

diurnal rhythm Daily time-patterns.

dualism Contrasted levels of development, wealth or well-being existing in close proximity to each other.

emergency aid Aid which is rushed to a region suffering from the effect of some natural disaster (e.g. earthquake) or man-made disaster (e.g. war).

emigration Moving *out of* one country to live in another.

fallow When exhausted land is left for the soil to recover it is fallow.

five-year plan Some countries produce long-term economic plans, which in China and USSR have five-year spans.

floodplain Flat land alongside a river, liable to flooding.

GNP See *gross national product*.

GNP per capita The GNP of a country divided by the population of the country.

green revolution Increase in food production by bringing new land into cultivation and raising crop yields by more scientific farming.

gross national product (GNP) The value of the total output of a country, both goods and services.

growth pole A centre of investment and industrial development from which it is intended that new wealth and ideas will spread outward toward the margins.

hierarchy An arrangement of individuals or phenomena (towns, countries etc.) in order, according to their size or status (see *rank*).

image A mental picture.

immigration The movement of people *into* one country from another.

infant mortality The number of deaths before the age of one year as a ratio of the number of live-births. Usually expressed as deaths per thousand live-births.

infrastructure A basic network of communications, power and water supplies, transport links and termini, schools, hospitals and other installations needed before development can take place on a large scale.

inhospitable environment A hostile or unwelcoming environment.

isotype A graph using symbols of proportional size.

less developed country (LDC) A country which, according to certain measurements, has a low level of economic activity.

life expectancy The average length of an individual life in a given community.

mean (mathematical mean) The sum of a collection of values divided by the total number of those values (the 'average').

median (mathematical median) The middle value in a sequence of values.

migration The movement of individuals or groups from one place to another.

mode (mathematical mode) The most commonly occurring value in a given collection of values.

mongoloid One of the three main groups of people recognised by anthropologists: characterised by yellow or red-brown skin and straight hair, originating in Eastern Asia and the Americas.

national mean income The total earnings divided by the total earners in a country.

nationality The country to which an individual belongs by birth or adoption.

natural change (population) The change in the size of a population as a result of the difference between births and deaths.

negroid One of the three major groups of people recognised by anthropologists - characterised by black or dark skins and originating in tropical Africa.

net migration The difference between immigration and emigration.

nodal point Where a series of routes meet.

occupation The way an individual earns a living.

per capita income The total income of a community or nation divided by the total number of individuals in that community or nation.

periphery The poorer margins, distant from the centres of economic development.

population change The change in the size of a population over time.

population cohort A group of people who experienced a certain event (such as birth or marriage) during the same time.

population density The number of individuals as a ratio of the size of the area they occupy.

population pyramid A bar graph showing the age and sex structure of a population.

population size The number of people in a population.

population variable One of the characteristics which distinguish an individual or group (e.g. age, religion, class).

prosperity gradient A graph showing 'wealth' on the vertical axis and 'geographical distance' on the horizontal axis will reveal prosperity gradients.

prosperity profile The shape of a prosperity gradient graph.

race A population variable deriving from inherited physiological characteristics (see caucasoid, mongoloid, negroid).

range The difference between the absolute maximum and minimum values in a group of values.

rank The place of an individual in a sequence ordered according to size or importance, the largest or most important being first. See also *hierarchy*.

remote Distant, isolated.

scattergraph A graph with two variables (one along each axis) with values plotted as points on the graph.

self-sufficient Providing for one's own needs (whether an individual or a community) without external assistance.

shifting agriculture Moving to a newly-cleared field when crop yield falls due to soil exhaustion in the old field.

social class A division of people according to lifestyle.

subsistence farming Producing for home use rather than for commercial distribution.

swash An advancing wave imparting forward motion. This is applied both to waves breaking on a beach and also, by analogy, waves of wealth and new ideas into an underdeveloped region. See also *backwash*.

technology The use of tools and machinery of varying degrees of sophistication and complexity.

transhumance The movement of livestock farmers with their animals between two regions of different climate (e.g. between uplands in summer and lowlands in winter).

tribe A social unit of people sharing given characteristics and often related by blood, lifestyle and interdependence.

variable A value which is not constant but varies from place to place, one individual to another and one time to another.

Index

Acknowledgements

The author and publishers wish to acknowledge the following photograph sources:

Aerofilms p. 3, Anne Bolt p. 86 left; Austin J. Brown p. 50 right; Jim Brownbill p. 9 left; Camera Press pp. 46 top, 50 left, 74 left, 92; J. Allan Cash Ltd pp. 46 bottom, 62, 85 right, 86 right; Christian Aid p. 73; Colorsport p. 2; F.A.O. photo by Peyton Johnson pp. 36, 85 left, Sally & Richard Greenhill pp. 9 centre; Alan Hutchinson p. 55; Icelandic Embassy p. 74 top right; Margaret Murray p. 42; Oxfam p. 75; Society for Cultural Relations with USSR p. 74 bottom right; Swiss National Tourist Office p. 39; World Bank – Photo Ray Witlin p. 63; Front cover of 'The Population Explosion – An Interdisciplinary Approach'; Permission Open University Press p. 25.

The authors and publishers wish to thank the following who have kindly given permission for the use of copyright material:

The Controller of Her Majesty's Stationery Office for data and statistics derived from tables 1.1, 1.2, 5.4a and 5.4b and for a map based on figure 5.1 all in the *Demographic Review of Great Britain*, 1977 Series DR No. 1.
Faber and Faber Ltd. for an extract from 'The Waste Land' and from 'Choruses from "The Rock"' from *Collected Poems 1909–1962* by T.S. Eliot.
Leeds City Council for data and statistics from Population Surveys and *Census Atlas of Leeds* (Part 1) 1977.
Longman Group Ltd. for extracts from Fig. 6 from *Gross Population Density and Population Change: London*, and from *Gross Population Density Alternative Data for Birmingham, Bristol and Liverpool*.
The Open University for four population pyramids and the back cover illustration of D100 Unit 32–36 *The Population Explosion – an Interdisciplinary Approach*, © 1971 The Open University Press.
Penguin Books for a map from *Where the Grass is Greener* by E.M. Smith.
West Yorkshire Metropolitan County Council for statistics from *Facts and Figures* (1974) leaflet.
The World Bank for data from the *World Bank Atlas*, 1981.

The publishers have made every effort to trace copyright holders, but if they have inadvertently overlooked any they will be pleased to make the necessary arrangements at the first opportunity.

The authors would like to thank Mr R. L. Young and other members of the Northumberland Geography 14–18 consortium for the original idea of 'Barota' in chapter 10.